THE ANCIENT
OLYMPIC
GAMES

THE ANCIENT
OLYMPIC
GAMES

Judith Swaddling

THE BRITISH MUSEUM PRESS

Published by The British Museum Press
A division of The British Museum Company Ltd
46 Bloomsbury Street, London WC1B 3QQ

First published 1980
Second edition 1999
Third edition 2004

A catalogue record for this book is available from
the British Library

ISBN 0-7141-2250-5

Designed and typeset in Monotype Bembo
by Martin Richards
Cover design by Andrew Shoolbred

Printed in Slovenia by Prešernova Družba d.d.

PAGE 1 *Colossal Roman marble bust of Herakles, legendary founder of the Olympic Games, based on a Greek statue of c.325–300 BC, height 95 cm.*

PAGE 2 *Bare-back riders in a horse-race. Panathenaic amphora, c.480 BC.*

THIS PAGE *View of Olympia from the west, showing the hill of Kronos to the left, and the plain of the river Alpheios in the distance. The tall columns belong to the palaistra.*

CONTENTS

The Olympic Games are a unique link between the classical world and modern times. During the thousand years of their ancient life and the century or so of their modern existence, competitors and spectators alike have shared the same passions and aspirations: they have been united by a passion for sport, an exhilaration in human strength, power and achievement and the excitement of competition. The Olympic ideal then as now was to set aside political differences and to prevent unfair practices in order to stage the ultimate sporting event.

It is sometimes claimed that the modern Olympics are a far cry from their ancient fore-runners, but this book is full of parallels between the ancient and the modern Games. Then as now, the Olympics were attended by thousands of spectators, training was arduous, and winners became both heroes and celebrities. Olympic victories were and are a matter of national pride, but it is still the names of the individual winners that we remember most. In their time Milo of Croton, Theogenes of Thasos and Diagoras of Rhodes were just as famous as Jesse Owens, Mohammed Ali or Steve Redgrave.

Perhaps the major difference between the ancient and the modern Games is that now women, who were once excluded from the Games, compete in virtually all events.

It is over twenty years since the first edition of this book, which now has a new chapter chronicling the landmarks and highlights of the modern Games since their re-birth in Athens in 1896. Regrettably our view of the modern Olympics of the past two decades has been coloured by various kinds of scandal, but the evidence presented here shows that this was part and parcel of the ancient Olympics, too, yet they survived one thousand years. Ancient obsessions with the promotion of good health and diet for athletes will strike another familiar chord with the modern world. Comic incidents and anecdotes about sportsmen were popular even then. There is something in this book for all who are interested in ancient Greece, the Olympic Games and sporting achievement.

Anne

1 THE OLYMPIC GAMES: WHERE AND WHY?

There are enough irksome and troublesome things in life; aren't things just as bad at the Olympic festival? Aren't you scorched there by the fierce heat? Aren't you crushed in the crowd? Isn't it difficult to freshen yourself up? Doesn't the rain soak you to the skin? Aren't you bothered by the noise, the din and other nuisances? But it seems to me that you are well able to bear and indeed gladly endure all this, when you think of the gripping spectacles that you will see.

(Epictetus, 1st–2nd century AD, *Dissertations* 1 6.23–9)

Every fourth year for a thousand years, from 776 BC to AD 395, the pageantry of the Olympic festival attracted citizens from all over the Greek world. They flocked to Olympia, the permanent setting for the Games, in the early years coming in their hundreds from neighbouring towns and city-states, and later in their thousands by land and sea from colonies as far away as Spain and Africa. What drew them all this way to endure the discomforts which Epictetus records? The Games, of course, and perhaps no less the celebratory banquets that followed, but there was something more...

The Games were held in honour of the god Zeus, the supreme god of Greek mythology, and a visit to Olympia was also a pilgrimage to his most sacred place, the grove known as the Altis. There is no modern parallel for Olympia; it would have to be a site combining a sports complex and a centre for religious devotion, something like a combination of Wembley Stadium and Westminster Abbey.

Olympia is situated in a fertile, grassy plain on the north bank of the broad river Alpheios, just to the east of its confluence with the Kladeos, which rushes down to meet it from the mountains of Elis. In ancient times the area was pleasantly shaded with plane and olive trees, white poplars and even palm-trees, while vines and flowering shrubs grew thickly beneath them. Rising above the site, to the north, is the lofty, pine-covered hill of Kronos, named after the father of Zeus. Successive waves of peoples who passed through the area in prehistoric times each observed the sanctity of this hallowed area. Modern visitors to the site often express surprise that the Games were held in such a remote area, but in antiquity the river Alpheios was navigable, and Olympia was easily accessible both from the sea (it was about 15 kilometres from the coast) and by means of inland routes converging on the site. The hill of Kronos must always have been a conspicuous landmark in the surrounding terrain (see pp. 4-5 and plan p.14, 35).

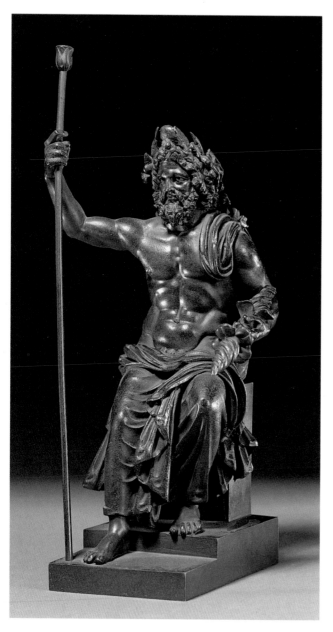

The clearing within the grove at the foot of the hill was once associated with fertility rites, for here was a very ancient oracle of Ge, the earth goddess. Gradually, as the worship of Zeus became predominant, people began to honour him at simple altars in the grove and hung their offerings – primitive terracotta and bronze figurines of men and animals – on the branches of nearby trees. With the establishment of the Games, this sanctuary grew and flourished. From the sixth century BC onwards the Altis was gradually adorned with temples, treasuries, halls, elaborate altars and literally hundreds of marble and bronze statues. The statues, some of which were several times life-size, were mostly victory dedications to Zeus for athletic and military achievements, and were set up by both states and individuals. There were also monuments erected in honour of benefactors, and offerings of costly materials given by wealthy tyrants and princes. Most remarkable of all the spectacles at Olympia was one of the Seven Wonders of the World: the resplendent 13-metre-high gold and ivory statue of Zeus within his magnificent temple. The statue was the work of Pheidias, the great sculptor of the fifth century BC.

As regards the origin of the Olympic Games, one can, as often in Greek history, either believe the legends, of which there are many, or look for a more down-to-earth beginning. According to the poet Pindar, Olympia was virtually created by Herakles, the 'superman' of Greek mythology. He made a clearing in the grove, laid out the boundaries of the Altis and instituted the

Bronze statuette of Zeus (Roman Jupiter), in whose honour the Olympic Games were held. Inside his temple at Olympia was a magnificent 13-metre-high, gold and ivory statue of the god. Although the statue was destroyed many centuries ago, its general appearance is known from contemporary descriptions and from representations on coins and small-scale versions like this. Roman, about 2nd century AD, height 18.4 cm.

Marble panel (metope) from the temple of Zeus at Olympia, in which the goddess Athena shows Herakles, legendary founder of the Olympic Games, where to breach the banks of the river Alpheios for the water to cleanse the lands of King Augeas of Elis. Augeas was said to have had so many oxen and goats that most of the country could not be cultivated for dung. This was the last of the Twelve Labours that Herakles had to complete in order to free himself from slavery to King Eurystheos of Argos. 468–456 BC, height 1.6 metres.

Herakles is received into heaven. A winged figure of Victory (Nike) presents him with a garland, and the god Zeus looks on, bearing his winged thunderbolt and sceptre. Herakles has his traditional attributes: a club, bow and lionskin. From an amphora made in Athens, c.475–450 BC.

This silver coin, with personifications of Olympia (top) and Zeus (above), was struck for the Games of 360 BC by the Eleans, who were the controllers of the Olympic festival. The legend 'FALEION' by Zeus's head means 'of the Eleans'.

first games in honour of Zeus. His purpose was to celebrate the success of one of his twelve labours, the cleaning of the cattle stables of King Augeas of Elis, which had been achieved by diverting the river Alpheios from its course. It is more likely, however, that athletic festivals like the Olympic Games developed from the funeral games that were held in honour of local heroes. Pelops, who will also be mentioned later, was the local hero of Olympia, and his grave and sanctuary were situated within the Altis. It is interesting that he was said to come from the east, for many people believe that it was in Asia Minor that the first organized athletic contests took place, when the Greek communities established there became prosperous enough to devote their leisure time to sport. At that time mainland Greece was still unsettled by wars and migrations.

The traditional date for the establishment of the Olympic Games was 776 BC, but competitions appear to have been held on an unofficial basis long before this. King Iphitos of Elis, a shadowy figure who lived around the ninth century BC, is said to have reinstituted the Games on the advice of the Delphic Oracle. The king had asked the Oracle how to bring an end to the civil wars and pestilence which were gradually destroying the land of Greece, whereupon the priestess advised that he should restore the Olympic Games and declare a truce for their duration. Whether this is true or not, the Olympic Truce was a major instrument in the unification, albeit temporary, of the Greek states and colonies.

Bronze tablet from Olympia recording an alliance between the Eleans and the Heraians of Arcadia for one hundred years, and stating that any offender against the agreement must pay one talent of silver to Zeus at Olympia. The efficacy of the Sacred Truce depended largely upon the maintenance of neutrality by the Eleans, which was achieved in part by treaties established with other city-states. About 500 BC, height 10.2 cm.

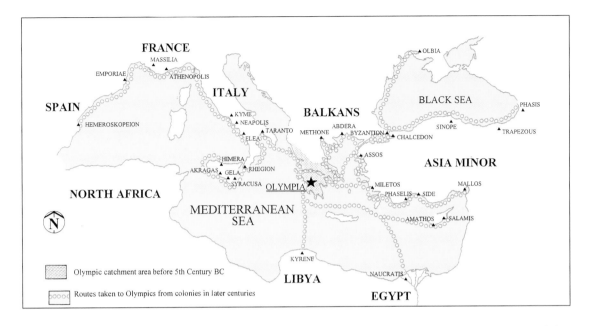

Map of the Mediterranean showing the Greek colonies from which competitors came in the 5th century BC to take part in the Olympic Games. For many centuries only citizens of Greece and the Greek colonies were allowed to compete.

In order to spread the news of the Truce before the beginning of the Olympic festival, three heralds decked with olive wreaths and carrying staffs were sent out from Elis to every Greek state. It was the heralds' duty to announce the exact date of the festival, to invite the inhabitants to attend and, most important of all, to announce the Olympic Truce. In this way they came to be known as the truce-bearers, *spondophoroi*; they served not only as heralds but also as full-time legal advisers to the Eleans. Originally the Truce lasted for one month but it was extended to two and then three months, to protect visitors coming from further afield. The terms of the Truce were engraved on a bronze discus that was kept in the Temple of Hera in the Altis. It forbade states participating in the Games to take up arms, to pursue legal disputes or to carry out death penalties. This was to ensure that pilgrims and athletes travelling to and from Olympia would have a safe journey. Violators of the Truce were heavily fined, and indeed on one occasion Alexander the Great himself had to recompense an Athenian who was robbed by some of his mercenaries whilst travelling to Olympia.

The Olympic Games were the oldest of the four panhellenic or national athletic festivals which composed the *periodos*, or 'circuit' games. The other three were the Pythian Games at Delphi, the Isthmian Games at Corinth and the Games at Nemea. Nowadays, a rough parallel for the big four events, as far as British athletes are concerned, would be the Olympics, the World Championships, the European and the Commonwealth Games. Then, as now, an athlete would try to win in all four; if he did, he was a *periodonikes*. Diagoras of Rhodes was one, and Daley Thompson, the decathlete, is an example of his modern counterpart. A major distinction between the Greek games and our own, however, is that all major and minor athletic festivals, of

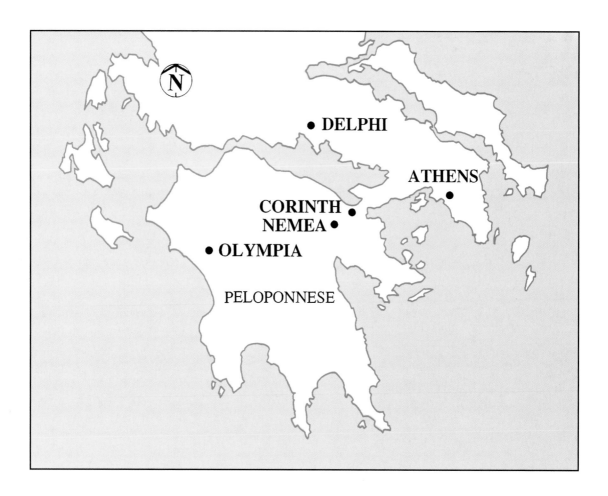

DELPHI

ATHENS

CORINTH

NEMEA

OLYMPIA

PELOPONNESE

Map of Greece showing the locations of the four major athletic festivals in Greece known as the periodos, *or 'circuit' games. Important games were also held at Athens as part of the Panathenaic festival, but this was a local event. Over the centuries hundreds of other city-states established their own games, many modelled on the Olympics; some of these even negotiated with the Eleans the right to entitle their games 'Olympic'.*

which several hundred had been established by Roman times, were celebrated under the patronage of a divinity. At Delphi Apollo was honoured; at Corinth, Poseidon and Nemea, as at Olympia, Zeus was the patron. The gods were believed to bestow on athletes the physical prowess that enabled them to take part in the Games, and accordingly athletes prayed to the relevant deity and promised offerings should they be victorious.

The Olympic festival was celebrated once every four years in accordance with the Greek calendar, which was based on the lunar month. It was always timed so that the central day of the festival coincided with the second or third full moon after the summer solstice. This may well indicate the assimilation at some stage of the Games with fertility rites that celebrated the harvesting. It is often asked why the Greeks should have chosen the very hottest time of the year, mid-August or mid-September, for such strenuous exertion. Apart from the lunar associations, it made sense to hold the Games at the one time during the year when work on the land was at a standstill; by then the crops were gathered and there was a lull in which men were eager to relax and celebrate the end of a hard year's work.

2 THE SITE

OUR SOURCES OF KNOWLEDGE FOR OLYMPIA

I f Olympia had not been rediscovered in 1766 by Richard Chandler, an English antiquarian and theologian carrying out an exploratory mission on behalf of the Society of Dilettanti, it is likely that the Olympic Games as we know them might never have existed. By attempting to follow the steps of Pausanias and also making enquiry of the local Turks, he found himself almost by chance in the Altis, which he identified, despite the almost total concealment of the site, from the remains of the walls of the Temple of Zeus.

It is ironic that Olympia, which was chosen for its strategic site, should be destroyed by natural forces peculiar to the locality. In the fourth century AD the river Kladeos burst its banks, destroying almost half the gymnasium and

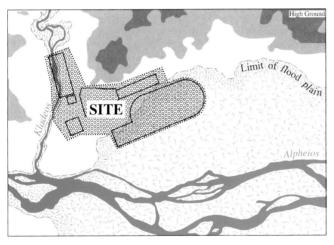

LEFT *Map of Olympia and the areas to the south and west of it, which were prone to frequent flooding from the converging rivers Kladeos and Alpheios. By the Middle Ages earthquakes, followed by floods, devastated the sanctuary and left it covered by several metres of silt.*

BELOW *The countryside around Olympia in 1806, sketched by the artist Sir William Gell, who was travelling with the archaeologist Edward Dodwell (seated right foreground). Although the hill of Kronos is conspicuous to the left in the distance, there is scarcely any indication of the sanctuary itself, lying below it to the right and still deep under the silt.*

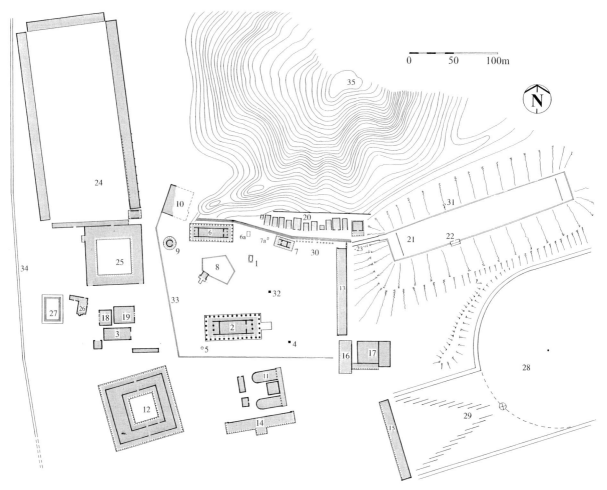

PLAN OF OLYMPIA C.100

1 Great Altar of Zeus	9 Philippeion	19 'Theokoleon'	29 Starting gate for
2 Temple of Zeus	10 Prytaneion	20 Treasuries	horse-races
3 Pheidias' workshop	11 Bouleuterion	21 Stadium	30 Zanes (statues of Zeus)
4 Statue of Victory by	12 Leonidaion	22 Judges' stand	31 Altar of Demeter
Paionios	13 Echo Colonnade	23 Entrance tunnel to	Chamyne
5 Sacred olive tree	14 Southern Colonnade	stadium	32 Pillar of Oinomaos
6 Temple of Hera	15 Colonnade of Agnaptos	24 Gymnasium	33 Altis wall
6a Altar of Hera	16 South-Eastern	25 Palaistra	34 Retaining wall of river
7 Temple of Rhea	Colonnade	26 Bathing facilities	Kladeos
7a Altar of Rhea	17 'Greek building'	27 Swimming pool	35 Hill of Kronos
8 Pelopion	18 Heroon	28 Hippodrome	

OPPOSITE ABOVE *View from the west of the British Museum's model of Olympia (compare the modern view, pp. 4–5). This model reproduces on a scale of 1:200 the buildings, monuments and landscape as they would have appeared in c.100 BC before extensive building work and alterations were carried out by the Romans. The building shown here in the centre is the* palaistra *with the gymnasium and its large courtyard on the left; the Temple of Zeus also features prominently to the right, above.*

OPPOSITE BELOW *Aerial view of Olympia from the south-west. The square building in the right foreground is the Leonidaion.*

never returning to its former course, and winter storms deposited rocks and earth from the nearby hill of Kronos across the sanctuary. In the sixth century AD two massive earthquakes tore the sanctuary apart, toppling the columns and shattering the walls of the most hallowed precinct of antiquity, and making the entire area uninhabitable. In the late Middle Ages the river Alpheios, flowing in the south, also flooded the sanctuary, washing away the hippodrome. As a result the entire site was covered with silt to an average depth of 4 metres, and the location of the sanctuary was forgotten.

Some four hundred years later, in 1829, a team of French archaeologists investigated the site, but it was not until 1875 that full-scale excavations were carried out by the German government, with the consent of the Greek authorities. King Friedrich-Wilhelm IV and his nephew Prince Friedrich-Wilhelm had been entranced by the vision of Olympia ever since hearing a lecture in 1852 by the eminent archaeologist Professor Ernst Curtius. The King was sufficiently moved to sponsor investigation of the site, and the subsequent excavations, which lasted six years, took place under the direction of Professor Curtius. With characteristic speed and efficiency the Germans regularly published the results of their findings.

The reports inspired Pierre de Coubertin, a French nobleman who had become obsessed with the athletic ideal of Olympia. Largely due to his enthusiastic efforts the first modern Olympic Games were held in Athens in 1896, where a magnificent marble stadium had been reconstructed for the occasion. Coubertin believed that the Olympic ideal would inspire amongst nations a competitiveness and team spirit unknown to the modern world. In fact the Greek ideal had been the physical excellence of the individual rather than the state, and the celebration of this gift in honour of the god.

In 1936 the German Institute of Archaeology began systematic excavation of Olympia, and to this day together with the Greek Archaeological Service they continue to reveal the reality of the myth. In the following description of the site the numbers accompanying the names of the buildings and monuments refer to those used in the plan on p.14.

Reconstruction of the Great Altar of Zeus, where one hundred oxen, a gift from the people of Elis, were sacrificed to Zeus on the middle day of the Olympic Festival.

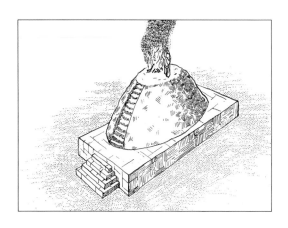

RELIGIOUS AND CIVIC MONUMENTS

1 Great Altar of Zeus

The altar is believed to have existed as early as the tenth century BC. According to legend, it marked the spot struck by a thunderbolt that Zeus hurled from his throne on Mount Olympos, when he laid claim to the area as his sacred precinct. In Pausanias' time the altar consisted of a stone base surmounted by a conical pile of ashes, 7 metres high, accumulated from sacrifices made to Zeus. The ashes left from each sacrifice were mixed with water from the Alpheios. The resulting paste was then plastered on to the altar, and subsequently solidified, year by year increasing the overall height. Ash from sacrifices made on the Altar of Hestia in the Prytaneion (10) was also added to the mound.

Model of the Temple of Zeus. The akroteria, *the ornaments on the corners of the roof, are gilt bronze tripods and figures of Victory. The sculpture in the pediments was originally painted and the background was probably blue, but as the colours are uncertain they have not been included on the model.*

2 Temple of Zeus

This magnificent temple took ten years to build and was completed in 456 BC. It was financed by spoils taken by the Eleans from neighbouring tribes, who were predominantly worshippers of Hera and initially resisted the establishment of Zeus as the supreme deity.

The temple was designed by an architect named Libon, who came from Elis. It must have been a remarkable sight: there were thirty-four massive

RIGHT *Fallen column drums of the Temple of Zeus. The massive columns carved from the local conglomerate stone were 2.2 metres in diameter at the base and 10.4 metres high.*

LEFT *One of the 102 marble lion-head water-spouts that drained rain water from the roof of the Temple of Zeus. Thirty-nine have survived. Because they were so heavy, the spouts tended to snap off and had to be replaced over the years.*

The chryselephantine (gold and ivory) statue of Zeus, which stood over 13 metres high. Pausanias says that a spiral staircase to an upper floor in the aisles of the temple enabled visitors to take a closer look at the god. The image was reflected in a pool of oil which was intended to prevent the ivory of the statue drying out.

BELOW *Bronze coin of Elis from the Roman period (reign of Geta, AD 209–12) depicting a seated Zeus. The image has often been taken as a representation of the cult statue by Pheidias.*

columns, surmounted by mouldings painted with intricate patterns in glowing red, blue and gold. Over one hundred marble water-spouts in the form of lions' heads drained water from the roof, which was tiled entirely in Pentelic marble specially brought from the quarries near Athens. In later times twenty-one gilded shields, dedicated by the Roman general Mummius after he sacked Corinth in 146 BC, were hung above the columns.

Many fine sculptures adorned the temple. The pediments, or gables, depicted two legendary scenes: in the east Zeus presided over the preparations for the chariot-race between Pelops and Oinomaos (see p. 82). In the west a battle raged between two mythological tribes, the Lapiths and the Centaurs. Inside the porches, high up under the ceiling, were panels representing the twelve labours of Herakles, the legendary creator of the Olympic Games.

As with other Greek temples, it is difficult to establish exactly what took place inside. The temple itself was primarily a shelter for the cult statue of the god, rather than a place of worship. There were many other statues and offerings which must have given the interior the appearance of a museum. Entry to temples was often restricted to priests, but at Olympia, at least by the time of Pausanias, visitors were allowed inside to see the great statue of Zeus.

The god is seated on a throne. He is made of gold and ivory, and on his head is a wreath representing sprays of olive. In his right hand stands a figure of Victory also of gold and ivory… in his left hand is a sceptre, skilfully wrought from a variety of metals. The bird perched on the sceptre is an eagle. The sandals of the god are of gold, and so is his robe, which is decorated with animals and lilies. The throne is adorned with gold, precious stones, ebony and ivory; it is painted and carved with figures…
I know that the measurements of height and breadth of Zeus at Olympia have been recorded, but I cannot commend the men who took the measurements, for their information falls far short of the impression which the image makes on the spectator.
(Pausanias, 2nd century AD, *Description of Greece* v 11.1–2, 9)

This colossal figure, 13 metres high, was considered one of the Seven Wonders of the World. It required so much ivory that Philo of Byzantium claimed it to be the reason why nature had created elephants. The head was so near to the ceiling that critics jibed that if Zeus stood up, he would literally raise the roof. Pheidias, who had already made the gold and ivory figure of Athena for the Parthenon in Athens, designed the statue and supervised its construction in his workshop west of the Altis. It was hollow, supported by an armature of wooden beams. In the small building to the south-west of 'Pheidias' Workshop' clay moulds and numerous fragments of glasswork, including faulty castings, were found. There were also some sixty clay fragments for making sections of drapery for one large and one small figure; these were suitable for the impression of gold sheet and were almost certainly used during the construction of the Zeus and the small figure of Victory which he held. The gold sheet could then have been fixed to a wooden support.

In front of the statue was a rectangular pool which would have reflected the image, but its purpose was also functional: it contained not water but olive oil, which provided moisture to prevent the ivory from cracking. The officials who took care of the statue probably treated it with additional oil: they were known as 'burnishers' and were traditionally the descendants of

Pheidias. The ivory must nevertheless have deteriorated over the centuries, for in the second century BC the sculptor Damophon of Messene was summoned to carry out repairs to it.

The lifespan of the Zeus was just over 900 years, but it did not end its days at Olympia. An abortive attempt was made by the Emperor Caligula to remove the statue to Rome in AD 40, but architects warned the Emperor that it could not be moved without breakage. It was said that a scaffold was set up for the purpose, but that a raucous laugh suddenly emitted from the statue and terrified the workmen, who then fled. If there is any truth in the story, then the noise was more probably the creaking of the ageing and decaying beams of the armature, among which, according to the Roman writer Lucian (second century AD), there lived a colony of rats and mice.

At the end of the fourth century AD the statue was looted and taken to a palace in Istanbul, so escaping the burning of the temple some thirty years later, but later it too was destroyed by a fire which razed many of the buildings in Istanbul in AD 475 (see pp. 100-101). The statue had survived long enough, however, for an artist to utilize the bearded, seated figure of Zeus as the image for Christ Pantocrator. And so Pheidias' masterful image of a pagan god lived on as one of the most important symbols of Christianity.

3 Pheidias' Workshop

This impressive studio seems to have been built especially to reproduce the interior of the Temple of Zeus. There is some debate as to the height of the building, but it was of the same dimensions as the *cella* (the main chamber of the temple), and it was very probably here that Pheidias created the gold and ivory statue. In the fifth century AD the building was converted into a church. One of the most fascinating finds was a broken clay mug inscribed in Greek underneath the base, 'I belong to Pheidias', which has been dated to about 440–430 BC. Some have thought it to be a hoax, but the encrustation within the letters has been analysed and found to be ancient, providing an intimate link with the sculptor's days at Olympia – unless, perhaps, it was the product of an ancient souvenir trade!

Black-glazed mug, inscribed on the base pheidio eimi – 'I [am the property] of Pheidias'. 440–430 BC, extant height 7.7 cm.

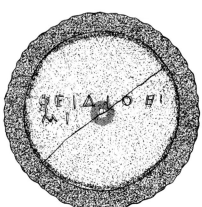

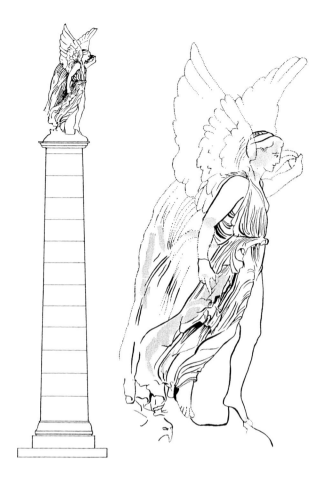

4 Statue of Victory by Paionios

This striking figure of Victory swooping down from the heavens was perched on top of a pillar 9 metres high, which still stands before the Temple of Zeus. The statue was said by Pausanias to be balanced on the back of an eagle in full flight, swooping down to her left, but it is now difficult to reconstruct the bird from the fragments. The eagle was the symbol and sometimes the personification of Zeus. The figure was originally brightly painted: her drapery was red, and her hair black, bound by a gold ribbon. It was dedicated by the Messenians, who, with their allies the Athenians, gained a momentous victory over the Spartans in the 420s BC, bringing a temporary halt to the Peloponnesian War.

The statue was made by Paionios of Mende. In the inscription on the base Paionios refers to his own victory in creating the *akroteria* (roof statues or ornaments) for the Temple of Zeus. This may refer to a competition for designs submitted by various artists, a common practice in antiquity to decide who should receive a commission.

5 Sacred olive tree

This was one of a number originally planted by Herakles, according to Pindar, and from it the Olympic crowns were made (see p. 90).

(see p. 90)

The Doric columns of the Temple of Hera, whose squat proportions are typical of early Greek temples.

6 & 6a Temple and Altar of Hera

This was the first temple to be built in the Altis in around 600 BC, and, save for the foundations of the prehistoric settlement in the north of the site, it is the oldest building at Olympia of which any remains survive.

It was probably erected by local tribes who paid homage to Hera, before the Eleans established Zeus as the sovereign deity in the Altis. There were two cult images in the temple, one of Hera and one of Zeus, the combination of the two statues symbolizing the union of religious beliefs between the two peoples. During excavations a limestone female head, twice life-size, was found west of the temple, but it very likely belonged to a sphinx and not to the statue of Hera.

The most remarkable feature of the temple was that no two of the columns were exactly alike, differing in style, thickness and type of stone. It appears that originally all the columns were made of wood, and were replaced one by one in stone as, over the years, they gradually rotted. They were probably not all removed at

Reconstruction of one of the painted terracotta akroteria which stood at either end of the roof ridge of the Temple of Hera; it is the oldest terracotta architectural element from Olympia. Early 6th century BC

Model of the north-western part of the Altis, with the circular Philippeion at the top, the Temple of Hera below it, the Temple of Rhea in the foreground and some of the Treasuries at bottom right. To the left of the Temple of Hera is the Pelopion, or burial mound of Pelops; in the time of Pausanias many statues stood among the trees in the enclosure.

once because it would be considered sacrilegious to remove any part of the temple unless absolutely essential. It is possible that each stone column was dedicated by a different person and this would account for the lack of uniformity. Originally only the foundations and lower parts of the walls were of stone; the upper walls were of mudbrick, and wooden rafters supported the terracotta roof-tiles. Winners in the Games of Hera, held for women at Olympia, dedicated paintings of themselves in the colonnade.

7 & 7a Temple and Altar of Rhea

The goddess Rhea was the mother of Zeus and wife of Kronos. The temple was built in the fourth century BC and its alignment was unusual, for the main facade was in the west, rather than the east as in most Greek temples. This may have been because it was considered essential that the temple faced the sacred altar, and the ideal site to the west was already occupied by the Temple of Hera. The Altar of Rhea had been in use for several centuries before a temple to her was erected. Altars were almost always situated in the open air, and worshippers made sacrifices at them, usually under the supervision of a priest.

8 Pelopion

Within this walled area was the so-called burial mound of the hero Pelops. Excavations have revealed a number of graves but there is no evidence to suggest a major burial. The graves date back to the third millennium BC, but the wall and grand entrance porch were not erected until the fifth or fourth century BC. Pausanias records that a shoulder-blade, believed to be that of Pelops, had been found there. For the possible significance of the tomb of Pelops for the origin of the Games, see p. 82.

9 Philippeion

This elegant building, roofed with carved marble tiles surmounted by a bronze poppy-head, was dedicated by Philip II of Macedon in celebration of both military and athletic victories. Philip had already won several chariot-races at Olympia, and his victories over the Greeks at Chaironeia in 338 BC presented the opportunity for a lavish dedication. He died only two years after the battle, and it is likely that his son Alexander the Great supervised the completion of the monument. Its circular shape is reminiscent of the beehive-tombs, called *tholoi*, which survive from the Mycenaean period. It may have been designed as a kind of cenotaph, especially as it housed statues depicting

Remains of the Philippeion. The three-tiered marble base is just over 15 metres in diameter, and the eighteen Ionic columns were coated in yellowish stucco.

Reverse of a silver tetradrachm minted in the name of Philip II of Macedon (359–336 BC) by one of his successors, probably at Amphipolis in c.323–316 BC. It presumably commemorates a victory by Philip at the Olympic Games in 356 BC; the rider holds a victory palm.

members of the Macedonian royal family. These were made from gold and ivory, materials normally reserved for images of the gods. The Altis wall (33) was laid out to incorporate the Philippeion within the sacred precinct, ndicating the desire of the Macedonians to establish themselves as cult figures in the Greek world.

10 Prytaneion

The many fragments of bronze vessels found during the excavation of this building support Pausanias' statement that it was the location of the great banquet given for victors in the Games. It was also an administrative centre for the cult and the festival. Built around 470 BC, it is believed to have housed the sacred fire of Hestia, goddess of the hearth, which was kept burning day and night, and from which a flame was carried to light the fires on all the other altars in the sanctuary. Winners in the Games received free meals and a seat for life in the Prytaneion. The poor condition of the foundations and the successive phases of building on the site have made this one of the most difficult buildings to reconstruct at Olympia.

11 Bouleuterion

The Bouleuterion, or Council House, was an ancient and venerable conglomeration of buildings. The south wing was constructed first, in around 550 BC, and was followed by the north wing, the central chamber and finally the colonnade in the east. The apsidal shape of the wings was a traditional design, originating several centuries earlier. The Olympic council held their meetings here, and the archives were possibly kept in the semi-circular storerooms at the end of each hall.

The statue of Zeus Horkios, in front of which Pausanias says the athletes, their relations and trainers swore the oath at the beginning of the festival, stood in the Bouleuterion, probably in the central room. For the oath, see p. 39.

View of the model looking north with the Leonidaion in the foreground, Pheidias's workshop behind it, and the palaistra and the gymnasium beyond.

12 Leonidaion

This was a hotel for visiting officials and VIPs. It was built in the fourth century BC at the expense of a certain Leonidas of Naxos, after whom it was named. It comprised numerous guestrooms and apartments for visitors who could stroll in the outer colonnade, which ran right round the building, and the inner colonnade, which looked on to the courtyard. There were probably trees and flower-beds in the courtyard, but the Roman water-gardens have destroyed any evidence that may have existed for their layout (see aerial view, p. 15).

13 Echo Colonnade

Constructed soon after the middle of the fourth century BC, this building strongly resembles the Philippeion (9) in its architectural style, and it has been suggested that Philip II dedicated both buildings. Situated along the eastern edge of the Altis, it formed a boundary that emphasized the separation of the stadium and hippodrome from the sanctuary.

Pausanias says that it was sometimes called the 'Painted Colonnade' because of the paintings on its walls. But it was usually known as the 'Echo Colonnade' as it echoed a man's voice seven times or more, and because of this the contests for heralds and trumpeters were held at the northern end. The narrow courtyard at the back was probably a store for athletic equipment (see model, p. 28).

14 Southern Colonnade

This elegant colonnade was built around 350 BC and would have provided a pleasant spot from which onlookers could watch the horses and chariots going to and from the hippodrome. At the start of the Games the *hellanodikai*, or 'Greek judges' (see p. 39), may have provided an official welcome under the projecting porch for the procession coming along the Sacred Way from Elis.

15 Colonnade of Agnaptos

Agnaptos constructed this building shortly after the Echo Colonnade was completed, but although Pausanias mentions it, there is now no trace of the structure, for any remains were swept away during flooding. It is believed to have stood at the back of the *aphesis* (the starting gate for horse-races: 29) and at right angles to the Southern Colonnade, so the space between the two colonnades probably served as an assembly area for horses and chariots.

16 South-Eastern Colonnade

The purpose of this building, constructed around 375 BC, is uncertain, although it may have been the *Hellanodikaion*, or 'Judges' Building'. The judges had another building in Elis where they prepared for the Games.

17 'Greek Building'

The uninformative title given to this building indicates our lack of knowledge about it. In early times there may have been a sanctuary of the goddess Hestia on the site, but the buildings later constructed there seem to have housed workshops.

18 Heroon

This building is known as the 'Heroon', as an altar dedicated to an unknown hero was found within it. Originally, however, it was a bath-house (see p. 34).

19 'Theokoleon'

This building, erected in the latter part of the fifth century BC, was for many years identified as the *theokoleon*, or 'Priests' House', where various religious officials could hold their meetings. Pausanias, however, indicates that the Priests' House was in the north near the Prytaneion, and the true identification of this building remains uncertain. As it is next to Pheidias' workshop, it may have provided living quarters for craftsmen or served as a store for the precious materials that they used.

20 Treasuries

The row of treasuries, each resembling a miniature temple, stood on a specially constructed terrace at the foot of the hill of Kronos (35). There were

ABOVE *Model of the Treasuries and the Echo Colonnade (right), with the Temple of Rhea to the left by the terrace wall, along which are the Zanes (statues of Zeus). Five of the Treasuries were set up by Greek colonies in Sicily and southern Italy (Selinus, Gela, Syracuse, Metapontum and Sybaris), the others by colonies at Epidamnos in Illyria, Byzantium on the Black Sea, and Kyrene in Northern Africa, and also by Sikyon and Megara on the Greek mainland.*

LEFT *Reconstruction of the entablature of one of the Treasuries, from a German excavation report. Most were decorated with painted terracotta panels and roof ornaments. They were built in the 6th century BC, the best preserved being the Treasury of Sikyon, which has been partially restored on site.*

eleven in all; the smallest structure, fifth from the right, was an altar. Each was set up by a Greek colony, wishing to gain prestige in their homeland. They housed objects of value, particularly those that needed shelter from the weather, and deposits of money, which the colonies could draw upon in times of need.

THE ANCIENT SPORTS COMPLEX

21 Stadium

The stadium did not exist during the early years of the Olympic Games. The athletes made use of an open level stretch of ground with a line drawn in the sand to mark the start (giving rise to the phrase 'starting from scratch'). As the races were held in honour of the god Zeus, it was appropriate that the finishing line should be close to his altar. The spectators stood on the lower slopes of the hill of Kronos.

These simple arrangements were adequate for the first centuries of the Olympic Games. Gradually various improvements were made and a rudimentary stadium was constructed within the Altis. It had shallow banks and a rectangular track, for all ancient races were run in a straight line. Eventually, around 350 BC a magnificent new stadium was constructed and it was situated, significantly, outside the Altis boundaries. By this time the games,

View of the stadium from the east, with the remains of the entrance tunnel at the far end. The slopes of the pine-clad hill of Kronos have subsided since antiquity, giving it a gentler less dramatic appearance.

although still part of the religious festival, had become established in their own right. Originally Zeus had been glorified for granting powers of strength and physical endurance to the athletes, but from at least as early as the fifth century BC, when there were about fifty other sports meetings besides the major Games, the athletes were becoming increasingly professional and beginning to gain recognition as cult figures themselves. Thus the removal of the stadium from the sacred precinct was a development in religious as well as athletic history.

The track in the stadium was of clay, levelled and lightly covered with sand. It had stone sills towards each end which marked the start and finish of the races (see pp. 60-61). To preserve some of the religious significance of the games it was desirable for all races to finish at the western end of the course, so that the runners still ran towards the heart of the Altis as they had done in the early days. Races consisting of an even number of lengths were therefore started at the western end. The course was separated from the embankment by a ridge of stone blocks, to the outside of which was a channel that conducted water round the stadium, discharging at intervals into basins for the refreshment of spectators who stood all day in the blazing sun without any shelter. There were no seats, and it has been suggested that the word 'stadium' was derived from the Greek word for 'to stand'.

The length of the track at Olympia is 600 Olympic feet, 192.28 metres. According to mythology, Herakles fixed the distance of the original race (and ultimately of the stadium) by placing one foot in front of the other six hundred times. An alternative explanation was that Herakles was able to run this distance in one breath before pausing to take another. All ancient stadia were approximately 600 feet in length, but with most places using a local standard of measure there was probably little concern for compatibility, which could account for slight variations in the length of each stadium.

Fragment of a bowl showing the chariot-race at the funeral games organised by Achilles for his beloved Patroklos (Achilles' name is on the right). Unlike the hippodrome and stadium at Olympia where the spectators stood on banks, the audience here sit on a two-sided, tiered stand where they are shown shouting and waving excitedly. The other inscriptions say 'Sophilos painted me' and 'Patroklos: the Games'. From an Athenian wine-bowl (dinos), 580–570 BC.

The ground rose naturally in the east, and artificial embankments were constructed in the north, west and south, requiring an immense amount of labour. In this way a surprising total of between forty and forty-five thousand spectators could be accommodated. To afford spectators an uninterrupted view of the race the two long embankments were designed so that they were 3 metres further apart at the centre than at the ends. This arrangement is found in other ancient stadia and was copied in the modern Olympic stadium in Athens (see p.102).

Up until the fifth century BC it had been the custom for rival Greek factions to set up trophies of arms and armour on the stadium banks, but when Greek

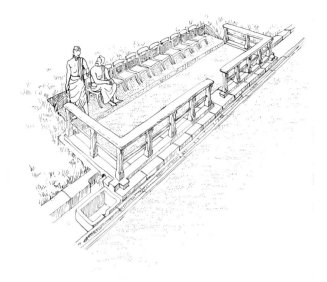

ABOVE *The judges' stand in the stadium. The space in front of the seats may have been used for the prize-giving ceremony, when perhaps the gold and ivory table for the wreaths was brought from the Temple of Hera. Apart from the foundations, no trace of the seats survives, and they have been restored on the basis of illustrations on vases.*

unity against Persian invasion became paramount, internal rivalry seems to have become distasteful and the practice was discontinued, here as in other Greek sanctuaries.

22 Judges' stand

A platform at the southern edge of the course, just under one third of the way from the western end, supported seats for the judges. Almost certainly those who were adjudicating a particular event would have stood at the finishing line and the seats were essentially honorary.

23 Entrance tunnel to stadium

The embankment at the west end of the stadium at Olympia required the construction of an entrance tunnel leading into the stadium from the Altis. This tunnel, which was 32 metres long with a vaulted roof, was the earliest example of such a structure in classical Greece. It was reserved for the use of judges and contestants only, and the western end of the tunnel could be closed by bronze trellis gates. The emergence into the stadium of the grand procession was a highlight of the festival. The tunnel was so well hidden beneath the earth embankment that Pausanias calls it the 'Secret Entrance'. Here the eager, anxious athletes must have waited to be summoned into the stadium for their particular contest. The tunnel into the stadium at Nemea is better preserved and tantalizing fragments of graffiti by known Olympic victors have survived, conveying a very human aspect of the games. One athlete wrote 'Akrotatos is beautiful', and another responded 'to the one who wrote it'.

LEFT *Remains of the stadium tunnel, looking east into the stadium.*

View from one of the rooms in the north-eastern corner of the palaistra looking west across the inner courtyard. The columns have been re-erected to give an idea of the general layout of the building. In the foreground, running behind a statue base, is one of the drains that form an intricate network across the site.

24 Gymnasium

This magnificent building was constructed during the second century BC. It is adjacent to the *palaistra* (see below) and both structures were probably for the use of competitors only. The great length of the gymnasium was determined by the fact that the eastern colonnade housed a double running track, 192.28 metres long, exactly the distance of the track in the stadium. This we know because sills similar to those in the stadium were found in place at each end of the colonnade. The athletes could practise here on a floor of levelled earth during excessively hot or rainy weather, and in order to warm up for their events in the Games. The courtyard of the gymnasium was large enough to accommodate additional running tracks and space for throwing the discus and javelin.

Around the middle of the second century BC the Eleans made an impressive addition to the gymnasium in the form of a majestic triple-arched gateway at the south-east corner. It must have been an imposing sight for those approaching the gymnasium from the northern entrance of the Altis.

No trace of the western half of the building remains today. In antiquity the river Kladeos was kept to its course west of the Altis by a retaining wall (34), but when it burst its banks and flooded the sanctuary in the fourth century AD, approximately half the gymnasium was swept away, including what Pausanias calls the living quarters for the athletes. The Kladeos never returned to its original course and today it forms the western limit of the excavated part of the sanctuary. The eastern end of the northern colonnade was detected during trial excavations before the Second World War, but the modern road and present usage of the area north of it hindered any further investigations.

25 *Palaistra*

Training in combat and jumping events took place in the *palaistra*. There was usually at least one *palaistra* in every city from the sixth century BC until the end of the Roman Empire. They were often privately owned, and people using the facilities were required to be members. It was not only a place for exercise but also a kind of social club, and just as it is customary now for friends to meet for a round of golf or a game of squash, then they would have enjoyed a bout of wrestling or boxing, followed by idle gossip or perhaps an intellectual discussion. According to Plato, Sokrates and Alkibiades were often to be found in a *palaistra* in Athens.

The *palaistra* at Olympia, which was built in the third century BC, followed the standard design for this type of building. It was a courtyard surrounded by four colonnades, at the backs of which were a number of rooms. Vitruvius, the Roman architect, wrote down the specifications for a *palaistra*, and with the aid of his information and the evidence of the excavations, it is possible to identify the use of most of the nineteen chambers. An oiling-room, called an *eliothesium*, and a powdering room, called a *konisterium* (see p. 73), opened off from the *ephebeium*, a common room for athletes in the centre of the north wing. This was the only room to have a marble floor; the rest had tamped-down soil or clay. The *ephebeium* also had access to the gymnasium.

At the eastern end of the north colonnade was a spacious cold bath and at the western end, a washroom. The bathing arrangements in a *palaistra* were usually more elaborate but at Olympia the athletes were already well provided with separate facilities for this purpose (see p. 34).

One of the main functions of the *palaistra* was to offer indoor facilities for the athletes during bad weather. All of the rooms except two, one in the west and one in the east wing, had benches all round for spectators. The exceptions are likely to be the *coryceum*, an exercise room that housed a punchbag, and an indoor training area for wrestlers. The long room in the southern colonnade would have been ideal for jumping practice. Any indoor or outdoor activity could be watched from the colonnades.

The purpose of a tiled area in the northern part of the courtyard at Olympia remains a mystery. It is composed of fluted tiles save for a narrow strip of plain tiles running lengthwise down the centre. It has been suggested that this area may have been used as some type of bowling alley. On the face of it this seems unlikely; however, the discovery of a similar arrangement in the Baths at Pompeii, with two large stone balls still in place on the tiles, increases the likelihood of this identification.

26 Bathing facilities and water supply

Baths existed at Olympia as early as the fifth century BC. Their existence at this stage is a measure of the importance that the Greeks attached to bathing after exercise.

Until this time washing facilities for athletes at Olympia had been fairly primitive and they made do with cold water in the wash room of the *palaistra* or gymnasium. Before these buildings were constructed, the athletes had used water from wells and basins, but by the fifth century, despite opposition, better facilities were coming into vogue. Many people condemned the arrival of hot baths as a sign of weakness: Plato thought them fit only for the old and feeble, while Aristophanes complained that the athletes were deserting the *palaistra* and going to the baths instead.

The early installations in the west of the Altis contained hip-baths and a hearth where water could be heated. The building which later became the Heroon, or shrine of an unnamed hero, was also originally a bath-house, containing the earliest known Greek steam-bath. Water was heated in huge bronze cauldrons in the southern room, and steam was then created by plunging them into cold water in the circular pool. The room to the west of this was the *apodyterion*, or changing-room. By 100 BC, however, the steam-bath had fallen into disuse, the baths in the west had been demolished and in their place appeared something quite new in Greece at that time – a Roman-type bath with underfloor heating known as a hypocaust, providing both hot water and steam-baths.

The intricate system of drains and channels that honeycomb the site at Olympia is indeed as remarkable as the buildings themselves. Good drainage was essential since the area tended to be marsh-like in the wetter seasons. However, the availability of fresh water was always a problem, particularly since the Kladeos would recede considerably and stagnate during the summer. A small supply came from springs to the north, but the problem was not substantially alleviated until the second century AD, when the Roman millionaire, Herodes Atticus, constructed a magnificent fountain complex at the western end of the Treasuries.

27 Swimming pool

This modern-looking open-air pool was unique in Classical Greece. Built in the fifth century BC, it was 24 metres long by 16 metres wide and 1.6 metres deep (roughly half the size of a modern 'Olympic-sized' pool), with steps leading down into it from each side.

28 Hippodrome

The *hippodrome* (literally 'horse-track') at Olympia will remain the most enigmatic area of the site. Pausanias tells us that it was to the east of the Altis and south of the stadium, but by the Middle Ages the River Alpheios had flooded

RIGHT *One athlete helps another to rinse the dust and sand out of his hair. From a Greek drinking-cup, 475–450 BC.*

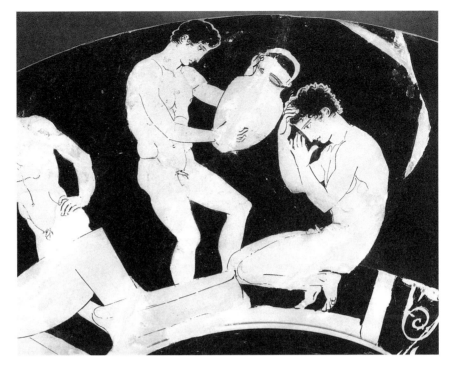

BELOW *Model of the swimming pool at Olympia, which at 24 metres long was just under the size of a typical modern public pool.*

its banks and completely washed away every feature in that area. To increase the difficulty of reconstruction, no other Greek hippodrome has left any informative remains. This is to be expected, as there was usually no special building associated with a hippodrome. An open stretch of level ground, often used at other times as grazing land, was all that was required. By preference it would be in a valley or at least at the foot of a hill to afford the spectators a good viewpoint. Usually there was seating only for the judges and perhaps a few privileged guests, while the rest of the spectators jostled with one another for the best vantage points. Artificial banks were often added later. A source of water in the immediate vicinity was essential to satisfy the thirst of both men and horses.

In the absence of any other evidence for the actual appearance of the hippodrome at Olympia, we must rely on surviving literary records; this entails gathering scattered references which range from a somewhat unsatisfactory description by Pausanias to measurements included in an eleventh-century manuscript found in the old Seraglio at Istanbul. The hippodrome was clearly on a larger and more elaborate scale than was customary. It is possible to estimate that the total length of the track was 600 metres (slightly over one-third of a mile) and that its width was in the region of 200 metres, sufficient to allow what appears to have been a standard line-up of about forty chariots – which might seem to us an enormous field. An average lap therefore would cover over 1,200 metres (just under three-quarters of a mile).

Pausanias says that the hippodrome was flanked by rising ground in the north and by an earth embankment in the south. For many years before the flooding this artificial bank served the dual purpose of accommodating the spectators and providing a barrier against the winter torrents of the Alpheios. We also know the approximate position of the judges' seats – to the western end of the northern bank, since Pausanias recalls arriving at them after clambering over the south bank of the stadium. This chance comment shows the fortuitous nature of our sources of knowledge for the hippodrome.

Two pillars were erected on the course to mark the turns; the one in the west also served to indicate the start and finish. In some of the scenes on pottery depicting horse-races this marker appears to be a portable wooden column, which is occasionally shown knocked over. However, at Olympia it was a permanent structure, surmounted by bronze statues representing Hippodameia crowning Pelops (see p. 82). Surviving representations of Greek horse-events do not illustrate the barrier that extended between the pillars or cones marking the turns on Roman race courses.

No doubt some kind of barrier ran round the perimeter of the track to protect the crowd from bolting horses or chariots careering out of control. There would have been gates in the barrier, for the removal of wreckage and injured parties.

The most remarkable feature of the hippodrome at Olympia was the starting apparatus, called the aphesis. This elaborate mechanism was much admired in antiquity. It was designed by Kleoetas, son of Aristokles, about whom unfortunately we know nothing, other than that he was proud enough to boast on the base of his statue in Athens that he invented 'the way of starting for the horses at Olympia'. The only surviving description of the apparatus is to be found in Pausanias' *Description of Greece*, VI 20.10–13:

The starting place is shaped like the prow of a ship, the beak being turned towards the course… At the very tip of the beak is a bronze dolphin on a rod. Each side of the starting place is more than four hundred feet long, and in each of the sides, stalls are built. These are assigned to the competitors by lot. In front of the chariots or race-horses stretches a rope as a barrier. An altar of unburnt brick, plastered over on the outside, is made every Olympiad as nearly as possible to the middle of the prow. On the altar is a bronze eagle, with its wings spread to the full. The starter sets the machinery in the altar going, whereupon up soars the eagle into the view of the spectators, and down falls the dolphin to the ground. The first ropes to be let go are those at the furthest ends of the prow, and the horses stationed here are the first off. Away they go until they come neck and neck with the chariots that have drawn the second stations. Then the ropes at the second stations are released. And so it runs on till all the chariots are abreast of each other at the beak of the prow. After that it is for the charioteers to display their skill and the horses their speed.

Schematic representation of the aphesis, or starting apparatus, in the hippodrome; in reality there were probably some forty traps for horses and chariots. According to Pausanias, there were many altars in the vicinity.

The general principles of the *aphesis* are clear, but there are insufficient details to make a definite reconstruction. We do not know how many competitors took part; Pindar was commissioned to write an ode in honour of Arkesilas, King of Cyrene, who won the chariot-race at Delphi in 462 BC where forty entrants competed; out of the forty, his charioteer Karrhotos was the only competitor to reach the finishing post with his chariot unscathed. Karrhotos dedicated the chariot at Delphi in thanksgiving, and on Arkesilas' return home with his victorious horses the ode was sung at the palace in his honour. The *aphesis* at Olympia was apparently designed both for spectacle and to achieve a staggered start: it allowed those horses starting at the outer edge, who had to travel further to reach the tip of the prow, an advantage of headway proportionate to their distance away from the centre. This ostentatious arrangement provided the sight of pent-up horses and colourful chariots successively bursting forth from their traps, and battling for the lead right from the very start.

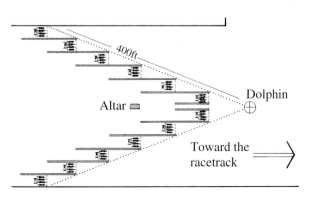

400ft

Altar

Dolphin

Toward the racetrack

3 RECORDS AND REGULATIONS

OUR SOURCES OF KNOWLEDGE FOR THE GAMES

We have no manual of Greek athletics; it is evident that in antiquity trainers could refer to textbooks containing exercises for physical prowess, but unfortunately only a few fragmentary passages on scraps of papyrus have survived. In addition, despite the passion for sport in antiquity, there seems to have been virtually no attempt to keep records of sporting achievements (see p. 63).

Luckily other sources do exist, and many will be referred to in the following pages. Most informative are the scenes represented on contemporary pottery, as the Greeks decorated a great many of their vessels with aspects of daily life. Another source of information is the coinage of certain city-states, depicting a sport at which they excelled. Furthermore a number of statues of athletes still exist, although most are Roman copies of Greek originals. It was customary for statues to record the achievements of successful athletes at the Games; many were of bronze, as this was believed to be the most durable of materials, but sadly in later years the value of the metal caused the statues to be melted down for other uses. Marble survives better than bronze although it can be broken up for building material or burnt to provide lime for mortar. Through the course of the centuries thousands of statues were plundered from Greek sanctuaries, many to be included in the collections of Roman aristocrats, but the vast majority were ultimately destroyed. Often only the statue-bases have survived, and from the inscriptions on them it is possible to glean a few details about the athletes who were commemorated and the events they won. Other official inscriptions provide some of the regulations for the athletic festivals and details about the officials who were in charge of them.

Finally, there are the literary sources. Contemporary Greek literature contains a number of incidental references to the Games, notably the Victory Odes of Pindar and Bacchylides, which were composed to honour the athletes of their day. There is also written information from the Roman period, which must be studied with caution when it refers to events which took place several hundred years before the time of the writer. Nonetheless these are invaluable documents since it is unlikely that the events changed a great deal over the years because of religious conservatism. The most prolific writer on the Olympic festival and on the site was the Greek geographer Pausanias, who in the second century AD wrote a detailed guide to Greece, compiled from his own travels. Another lengthy text survives from a treatise *On Gymnastics* by Philostratus of Lemnos, who wrote during the second and third centuries AD. It contains some interesting details, but sadly the author appears to have had little, if any, practical experience of athletics himself, and the book was probably written as an intellectual exercise. Very little survives of the official lists of victors. Part of the list of winners in the foot-race survives, as an extract was incorporated into a Roman work of the fourth century AD, and by chance the names of some of the victors from the fifth century BC have been preserved on the back of a Roman financial account. These are the pieces of information that must be fitted together like a jigsaw puzzle to provide a picture that, although incomplete, is sufficient to show what the Games were like in antiquity.

RULES

But the Zeus in the Bouleuterion is of all the images of Zeus most likely to strike terror into the hearts of sinners. He is surnamed Horkios [Oath god] and in each hand he holds a thunderbolt. Beside this image it is the custom for athletes, their fathers and their brothers, as well as their trainers, to swear an oath upon slices of boar's flesh that in nothing will they sin against the Olympic Games . . .

(Pausanias, 2nd century AD, *Description of Greece* v 24.9–10)

Bezel of a cast gold ring with a very rare depiction of a statue of Zeus Horkios (Zeus of the Oaths), before whom the Olympic oath was sworn. The god is identified by the unusual feature of having a thunderbolt in either hand, and by a flaming altar and a boar, which was sacrificed for the ceremony. About 325–275 BC.

This quotation refers to the oath taken by the athletes at the start of each Olympic festival. In addition the *hellanodikai* (judges) had to swear that they would judge fairly and treat in confidence anything that they had learned about a competitor. They were entirely responsible for the enforcement of rules and regulations and acted as both judges and umpires; they also meted out punishment for any infringements. The penalties were harsh: both competitors and trainers who failed to comply with instructions could be publicly whipped by the *mastigophorai* (whip-bearers), a form of punishment usually reserved for slaves. Thucydides reports that the Spartan Lichas, who registered as a Theban to enter the chariot-race because the Spartans were currently banned from the Games (see p. 99), was publicly whipped for his dishonesty.

Heavy fines were occasionally imposed, especially in cases of bribery, which was regarded as a particularly odious crime. As a warning to potential offenders money from such fines was used to pay for bronze statues of Zeus (known as *Zanes*, a dialect form of Zeus), which were set up along the terrace wall leading to the entrance of the stadium (plan p. 14, 30; model p. 28). According to Pausanias, there were sixteen of these in all, six of which were erected from fines levied on the city of Athens, when Kallipos, an Athenian, bribed his opponents in the pentathlon. Athens refused to pay until the Delphic oracle threatened that there would be no more prophecies unless the

A seated official who may well be a judge, since a starting or finishing post stands behind him. From a Greek amphora (storage-jar), 475–450 BC.

fine was paid in full. Instances of bribery were relatively rare, and Pausanias remarked that it was incredible for any man to have so little respect for the god and even more incredible 'that one of the Eleans themselves should fall so low'. This was Damonikos, the parent of a boy athlete who was over-anxious for his son's success. He had bribed the father of his son's opponent, and on discovery both the fathers were fined.

It must often have been difficult to decide the winner, particularly in the foot- and horse-races, where the judges had to rely on eyesight; there was of course no such thing as a photo-finish. In the event of a draw the crown was dedicated to the god. There was only one victor; coming second or third counted for nothing. Pindar described how a defeated athlete would slink home via back-alleys 'smitten by his misfortune'. By contrast, nowadays, silver or bronze medallists, even those defeated in the first round of the heats, are regularly praised – although a notable exception was a competitor from Japan in the 1964 Tokyo Olympics who after finishing second in the marathon killed himself because of his sense of shame at not having won.

WOMEN AT OLYMPIA

On the road to Olympia…there is a precipitous mountain with lofty cliffs… the mountain is called Typaeum. It is a law of Elis that any woman who is discovered at the Olympic Games will be pitched headlong from this mountain.

(Pausanias, 2nd century AD, Description of Greece v 6.7)

Apparently this ban applied only to married women, as Pausanias states elsewhere that 'virgins were not refused admission'. No written evidence survives to explain this discrimination, but it is possible that the practice dated back to the fertility games of the remote past when only virgins were considered pure enough to attend the sacred rites. If this was the original reason, then it had been long forgotten, for Dio Chrysostomus says that 'even women of dubious character' were allowed at the panhellenic games.

There was one married woman who was actually required to witness the Games; she was the priestess of Demeter Chamyne. The marble altar of the goddess (plan p. 14, 31) was situated halfway along the north bank of the stadium, and on this the priestess sat to observe the Games. Demeter was the goddess linked with vegetation and fertility, and the epithet *Chamyne*, meaning 'of the couch', may again refer back to some fertility ritual. This would have been before the Games were established in honour of Zeus.

Only one other married woman is known to have gained admittance to the Games. She was called either Kallipateira or Pherenike, and she was the daughter of Diagoras, the famous boxer from Rhodes (p. 81). As her husband was dead, she disguised herself as a trainer and brought her son Pisirodos to Olympia to compete. Pisirodos won, and in her excitement the mother leapt over the barrier of the trainers' enclosure and in so doing exposed herself. But the authorities let her go unpunished out of respect for her father, brothers and son, all of whom had won Olympic victories. As a precaution, however, they passed a law that in future the trainers, like the athletes, must be naked when they came to be registered.

Women themselves were definitely not allowed to compete in the Olympics, but this did not prevent them from participating indirectly. As owners of horses, they could not be prevented from entering their teams in the chariot events, and several women are known to have done this at Olympia. The first and most famous of all was Kyniska, daughter of King Archidamos of Sparta. Plutarch, the Greek biographer who lived in the first and second centuries AD, says that her brother Agesilaos persuaded her to enter a chariot in one of the races, in order to prove that victory in equestrian events was a result of wealth and nothing to do with skill.

But, according to Pausanias, Kyniska had always had one great ambition – to win an Olympic victory. This she achieved, and in celebration of the event she set up two bronze monuments representing chariots, a small one in the antechamber of the temple of Zeus, and a larger one in the grounds of the Altis. Part of the inscribed base of the larger monument has been found and indicates that it included a statue of her. An ancient source recorded the full wording of the inscription:

> Sparta's kings were fathers and brothers of mine,
> But since with my chariot and storming horses I, Kyniska,
> Have won the prize, I place my effigy here
> And proudly proclaim
> That of all Grecian women
> I first bore the crown.
> (*Greek Anthology* XIII 16, after Drees)

THE GAMES OF HERA

Bronze statuette of a girl runner, probably from Sparta, where women were expected to take part in athletics. Her appearance corresponds well with Pausanias' description of the girls who raced in the Heraia: 'Their hair hangs down, a tunic reaches to a little above the knee, and they bare the right shoulder as far as the breast.' (Description of Greece V 16.4). About 500 BC, height 11.4 cm.

Women were excluded from competing in the Olympic Games, but they did have a festival of their own at Olympia. This was the Heraia, or games held in honour of Hera. These were also celebrated every four years, but there was only one type of event – the foot-race. It was divided into three separate contests for girls of different age-groups. Pausanias provides details about the organization of these games, which were the responsibility of sixteen of the most respected women of Elis, each aided by an assistant. This tradition was traced back to the wedding celebrations of Hippodameia, who chose sixteen matrons to help her inaugurate the Heraia (see p. 82).

The track in the stadium was shortened by one sixth especially for the contests, making it just over 160 metres. This is a strange alteration, as one would imagine that any woman who could run 160 metres could equally manage 180. Perhaps the difference reflects not difference in physical ability but the Greek male view that women were by nature inferior to men. The winners were given crowns of olive like the Olympic victors, and they also received a portion of a heifer sacrificed to Hera. Just as the Olympic prize-winners were allowed to dedicate statues of themselves, so the girl victors were granted the privilege of setting up their images in the temple of Hera. Evidence suggests that these were paintings rather than statues.

Religious conservatism is probably the reason why no other competitions were ever introduced for women at Olympia, even though by the Christian era most of the major Greek games incorporated women's events. It should, however, be remembered that although women were allowed to compete in the modern Olympic Games from 1900, the number of events in which they participitated was strictly limited: in 1900 there was only tennis, which was replaced in 1904 by archery. Gradually the contests open to women increased, although for many years the longest running event was the 3,000 metres, and it was not until 1984 that the women's marathon was introduced into the programme. At Sparta girls seem always to have undertaken the same athletic exercises as boys, as tough, strong mothers were believed to produce good Spartan soldiers. Even Plato, composing the guidelines for his ideal state, advocated running and sword-fighting for women, but he stressed that after the age of thirteen they should wear 'appropriate dress'. It is curious that in Greece strigils, or scrapers (to clean off dirt and oil), which are often shown being used by male athletes, were rarely associated with women. But in ancient Etruria, where Greek cultural pursuits and sport were popular, women seem both to have used strigils and prized them sufficiently to have them buried along with other treasured possessions in their tombs. Women in Etruria, however, played a much greater part in public life.

4 PREPARATION AND TRAINING

You say 'I want to win at Olympia'. But wait. Look at what is involved... You will have to obey instructions, keep away from desserts, eat only at set hours, in both heat and cold; you must not drink cold water nor can you have a drink of wine whenever you want. You must hand yourself over to your coach exactly as you would to a doctor. Then in the contest you must gouge and be gouged; there will be times when you will sprain a wrist, twist your ankle, swallow mouthfuls of sand and be flogged. And after all that there are times when you will lose.

(Epictetus, 1st–2nd century AD, *Discourses* 15, 2–5)

MEDICAL CARE

Good physicians have always been in demand in the world of sport. In antiquity their skills were crucial in view of the rigours and brutality of some of the events, and then as now it was important for athletes to be in peak fitness. Those with a genuine knowledge of healing and the workings of the human body contributed much to sport; it has even been suggested that the development of medical expertise in the Greek and Roman world was related to the evolution of sport, and virtually came to a standstill when the major Games ceased in the late fourth century AD. A mythical tradition associating sport and medicine held that Asklepios, the Greek god of medicine, learned his skills from the centaur Cheiron, who was credited with

Two boxers, one bleeding profusely from the nose. On their hands are thongs, or himantes. *From an amphora made in Athens, 550–540 BC.*

the introduction of competitive gymnastics and of music from the double pipes to accompany exercise. A rather more factual association can be found in the fact that one of the two surviving lists of Olympic victors is preserved in the writings of the philosopher Aristotle, son of Nikomachos, royal physician to Philip of Macedon.

Illustration from the Codex of Chirurgy, showing a patient being treated for a dislocated knee. The codex was a Byzantine copy (10th century AD) of an illustrated Roman version of Apollonios of Citrium's commentary (1st century BC) on one of the Hippocratic treatises.

Doctors and trainers

It is no surprise that one of the officials at the Games was a doctor and that the presence at sporting activities of what we might now call paramedics or first-aiders is well attested. Some of these were personal trainers: we know that at gymnasiums there were *gymnotribai* who taught athletic skills, and sportsmen who could afford it were likely to have employed their own specialist. *Gymnotribai* seem to have been considered as of equal importance to the *paidotribai* who were responsible for the educational and intellectual upbringing of their young charges, and it is interesting that in antiquity educational classes became adjuncts of the gymnasiums and *palaistra* rather than the other way around. Intellectual and physical education were inseparable. The two most famous gymnasiums in Athens were the Academy and the Lyceum, where Plato and Aristotle, respectively, taught. *Paidotribai* and *gymnotribai* are frequently shown in vase paintings instructing their protégés during exercise or events, or massaging them with oil. Some were called simply *aleiptai*, or massagers, while others became *iatroleiptai*, healer-massagers, or *hygienoi iatroi*, something like fitness specialists, and they seem to have combined a knowledge of physiotherapy and diet. They were able to deal with minor injuries like a shoulder dislocation, for which Hippocrates describes a simple method of reduction, recording it as being useful in the *palaistra*. The range of treatments available to physicians in antiquity is impressive. They could deal with all kinds of fractures using various splints and bone-cutters; they employed complex bandaging and

A man leaning on a stick having his heel bandaged. In this instance the characters are the doctor Machaon, son of Asklepios, and Philoctetes, who is being treated for a snake-bite, but injuries to bare feet must have been common in ancient sport. Etruscan carnelian scarab-shaped sealstone, 5th century BC, 1.9 x 1.5 cm.

stitched wounds; and they operated on skull fractures, removing fractured bone by drilling and occasionally trepanning. The major medical problems were infection, as there was no understanding of the bacteria which cause disease, and the lack of general anaesthetics.

Some athletes probably had a basic knowledge of the workings of the human body, such as Ikkos of Taras (Taranto) who wrote a treatise on athletics and may himself have won the pentathlon at Olympia in 444 BC. An approximate modern parallel would be the British Olympic runner Roger Bannister, a doctor who undertook a scientific method of training and studied the mechanics of running; in 1954 he became the first person to run a mile in under four minutes

There seems to have been a certain amount of rivalry between coaches and physicians. Philostratus, who wrote much about the Olympics and ancient athletics, discusses the intrusion of the athletes' trainers into medicine, and it was perhaps this meddling which coloured the attitude of Galen towards athletes. Galen (AD 129–199/216), a Greek physician whose theories concerning the 'humours' and the circulation of the blood dominated Western medicine for some 1,500 years, was himself a physician to gladiators and later the personal doctor of the Roman emperor Marcus Aurelius. In his treatise addressed to Thrasyboulos, 'Is health a matter of medicine or exercise?', he comments scathingly that failed athletes operated as healers and massagers and even attempted to write books on the subject. There was no doubt much scope for quacks and profiteers, and clearly money was to be earned in roles associated with sport, especially from professional athletes and at the large sporting events.

Hippocrates (c.460–380 BC), the father of modern medicine, advocated a holistic approach to health and healing which appeals to modern thought. He was a Greek physician from the island of Kos to whom were attributed some seventy works on health and medicine, though he was probably not directly responsible for writing them. Some of these works advocate concepts which are still attractive to us, cleanliness, moderation in eating and drinking, letting nature take its course, and living where the air is good. In the Hippocratic writings no reference is made to the actual Olympics, but there is frequent mention of diet, exercise and treatment of injuries which might be sustained in sport. Hippocrates is also credited with the discovery of aspirin in willow bark, renowned for its anti-inflammatory and analgesic properties. Beside a plethora of herbal remedies, minerals of a wide variety were popular in classical medicine. Galen in his *Composition of Medicines* gives a standard recipe for 'Olympic victor's brown ointment' to relieve strains, which he had modified with the addition of two ingredients: it included cadmium, opium, antimony, zinc oxide, frankincense, aloe indica, saffron, myrrh and a raw egg.

Diet and exercise

The paramount importance of diet and exercise was well recognized in antiquity. Vigorous dancing was noted for its all-round benefits, including even distribution of weight, unlike long-distance running, which was held to thicken the legs and weaken the shoulders, or boxing, which did the opposite. Galen recommended ball-playing as good general exercise, and other 'natural' activities such as digging and rowing. Hippocrates was perhaps the first to state the now often repeated maxim that those who wish to become slimmer must not only exercise but also monitor their food intake – to the point of fasting. Both Hippocrates and Galen, however, seem to have believed that athletes trained excessively and risked damaging their health; Galen went so far as to say that over-specialization in a particular type of event made athletes less effective as manual labourers and as soldiers.

Various types of diet were tried: in the early years dried figs, moist cheese and wheat were favoured, but then a trainer named Pythagoras (not the philosopher) recommended a meat diet. Meat was expensive, and its consumption became mainly the preserve of athletes: this was one reason why the banquet of roast ox at the heart of the Olympic festival was so special. Philostratus compared the diet favoured by athletes of 'older times' – bread made from barley, unleavened loaves of unsifted wheat, and the meat of oxen, bulls, goats and deer – with that of his contemporary athletes, with whom doctors were too easy-going, recommending white bread made from ground meal sprinkled with poppy seeds, copious quantities of fish (previously discouraged among athletes) and other 'fancy food', in effect turning athletes into 'gluttons with bottomless stomachs'. In general the diet of the classical world was frugal, based mainly on wheat, olive oil and wine, which was the main beverage, usually mixed with water. Hippocrates considered cheese to be 'a wicked food', though it was otherwise the major source of protein, as milk would not keep in a hot climate. To build bulk for gladiators, Galen recommended beans, which were acceptable provided that they were boiled long enough to avoid flatulence. Fruit and vegetables were important, and so was fish and other types of sea-food. Honey was used for sweetening, and herbs and spices were of course important for flavouring.

There were familiar arguments about the pros and cons of sexual activity during training. Some athletes like Ikkos, mentioned above, were said never to have touched woman or boy during their entire preparation for the games. Diogenes Laertius, who wrote *Lives of the Philosophers*, claimed that sex was always unhealthy and debilitating, but that it was less harmful in autumn and winter than in spring and summer. This does not seem to have deterred the general practice of older men to seek young lovers among the athletes in the gymnasium and *palaistra*.

A man using a strigil, or scraper. Etruscan bronze statuette, c.500 BC, height 10.7 cm.

Hazards and drugs

Besides sports injuries, competitors in the Games faced other hazards, such as the likelihood of sunstroke, given that they competed in the blazing sun at the hottest time of the year: Philostratus confirms that an ability to endure the sun was essential for an athlete. The risk of sunburn was probably lessened to some extent by the application of olive oil before contests or exercise: it was also used for massage by coaches or trainers, and was later scraped off with a strigil, which would have had a powerful toning effect. It is interesting that Herakles, mythical founder of the Games, had a therapeutic function in some of his cults, especially as a protector from heat: a recent study has compared the iconography of Herakles with that of Asklepios. Flies and mosquitoes presented another hazard, and the Eleans regularly worshipped Zeus Apomyios, 'Averter of Flies'. It was said that Herakles, when making a sacrifice at Olympia, was badly pestered by flies and either invented or was taught to appeal to Zeus in this capacity. Other risks perhaps encountered at Olympia were food-poisoning and infection from a water-supply that was highly likely to be contaminated. Tetanus and possibly malaria may well have prevailed at Olympia. Spectators, too, were prone to all of these ills: it is believed that the philosopher Thales of Miletos died from sunstroke at Olympia. There was also risk from being accidentally struck by a javelin or discus. According to tradition, Oxylus of Elis left his country because he accidentally killed his brother Thermios with a throw of the discus.

Aryballos and two strigils on a chain. Before exercise athletes would rub olive oil on their skin. The oil was kept in an aryballos, or small flask, which was often tied on to the wrist. The oil helped to prevent sunburn, and stopped dirt from getting into the pores. Afterwards a strigil was used to scrape off the oil and dirt. Roman, height 6.8 cm.

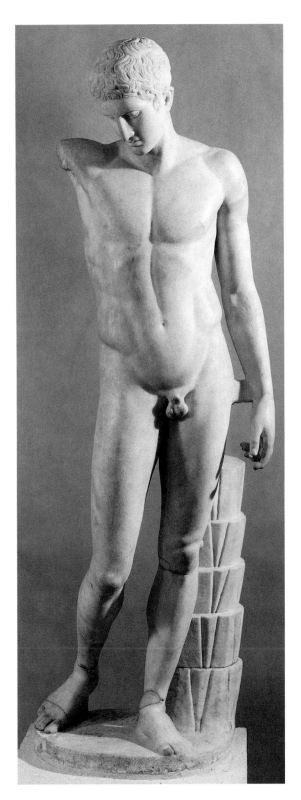

As for the use of performance-enhancing drugs in antiquity, a question now often asked, no evidence exists. One could argue that since herbal medication was freely used, including substances for mood and behavioural changes, it is doubtful that any treatments were actually banned. The use of pharmacology probably goes back to the Bronze Age, for there are references in both the *Iliad* and the *Odyssey*. We are told, for example, that Helen of Troy learned the use of sophisticated and efficacious drugs from Polydamna, a woman of Egypt, 'where the earth produces many drugs, both beneficial and troublesome' (*Odyssey* IV 219–32). Athletes participating in the festivities at Olympia would no doubt have welcomed the medicament given by Hermes to Odysseus, a powerful drug that prevented drunkenness and was made from *molu*, a plant with a black root and milk-white flower; it was said to be difficult to dig up, and is so far unidentified.

THE BUILD-UP TO THE FESTIVAL

If you have worked hard enough to render yourself worthy of going to Olympia, if you have not been idle or ill-disciplined, then go with confidence; but those who have not trained in this fashion, let them go where they will.

> (Philostratus the Elder, 2nd–3rd century AD,
> *Apollonius of Tyana* V 43)

The Olympic Festival lasted for five days but the preparations took virtually the whole of the preceding year. Strangely, there is no firm evidence that the sports facilities at Olympia were used

The 'Westmacott Athlete', a Roman marble copy of a Greek work of about 440 BC. The popularity of Greek works of art among the Romans, following the plundering of many cities and sanctuaries in Greece, led to the production of numerous copies. Height 1.5 metres.

during the period between the festivals. Local villagers may have exercised there but they would have been few in number. Much hard physical labour was therefore required to get things ready. Any undergrowth that had sprung up had to be cleared. The courses had to be dug and levelled and the sand pits prepared. Repairs and general tidying up of the buildings and monuments in and around the sanctuary were also necessary.

Nowadays, with the huge increase in the scale of the Olympics, the task of preparation is immeasurably greater still, billions of dollars and many years being required to get the designated Olympic city into suitable condition. For this reason in the early 1990s the idea was floated of returning the Olympics to a permanent site at Olympia, but it was soon realized that ancient Olympia could not possibly cater for the scale of the modern Olympic Games.

Ten months to go

The most important officials at the Games, who were known as the *hellanodikai,* commenced preparations ten months before the games were due to start. Their name means literally 'Greek judges', reflecting the national character of the Games. In the early years of the festival they had been referred to merely as *agonothetai,* 'games organizers'. They had their own special residence in Elis called the Hellanodikaion. The *hellanodikai* were chosen by lot, and although their numbers fluctuated, there were ten for most of the history of the Games. One of them acted as the overall supervisor while the rest were divided into three groups, each presiding over different events. The first group organized the equestrian events, the second the pentathlon, and the third the remainder of the competitions. Throughout the ages the Olympic judges were renowned for their impartiality (see, however, p. 98). They wore robes of purple, the royal colour, serving as a reminder of the time when King Iphitos controlled the Games and officiated as the sole judge.

The athletes, too, had to be in strict training in their home towns during the ten months prior to the Games and they had to swear an oath to this effect. This rule would seem odd for a modern athlete, since ten months of hard training, far from enabling an athlete to be at his or her peak at the end of the period, would be liable to have the opposite effect, leaving the athlete injured and exhausted. It suggests that by comparison with their modern-day counterparts, ancient Greek athletes started from a relatively low level of fitness and might be novices at their event.

One month to go

For at least one month before the festival prospective competitors in the Games were required to reside at Elis and train under the strict supervision of the *hellanodikai.* There were three gymnasia at Elis, and in addition the local market place was stripped and used as a practice track for the horse-races. This period of compulsory training at Elis was enforced by the Eleans probably to demonstrate their absolute control over the Games. Their authority had been

An instructor (right) supervises a training session. The discus-thrower is poised at the farthest point of his backward swing, while the athlete on the ground binds a thong around a javelin. Beside him are a pick, used for breaking up the pitch, and a pair of jumping weights. Rhythm is provided by a pipe-player whose cheeks are bound to prevent his face becoming disfigured. Shoulder of a water-jar, c.510–500 BC.

contested in the past particularly by their neighbours the Pisatans, but eventually the Eleans established supremacy (see p. 99). During this month the judges were fully occupied with various tasks: they disqualified those who were not fit, checked on parentage and Greek descent, and resolved any disputes concerning the classification of men and boys, horses and colts.

The training was renowned for its harshness: the athletes had to observe a strict diet, carry out a gruelling regime of exercise and obey every word of the *hellanodikai*. It is not certain when the period of compulsory training was introduced, but since it required the athlete to be away from home for a considerable time he had to be fairly affluent. Sometimes his father or brother would accompany him to Elis, but often a private trainer was employed. By this time the era of the amateur athlete was clearly coming to a close. Nowadays many athletes take their own coaches or trainers to the Games with them, and the idea of being compelled to adopt the training regime of an official, alien coach would not be very appealing.

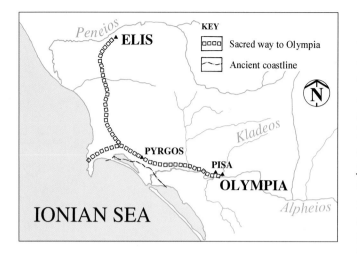

KEY

▫▫▫▫ Sacred way to Olympia

〰 Ancient coastline

Map of the Sacred Way from Elis to Olympia, a distance of about 58 kilometres, along which the judges, trainers and competitors set out two days before the Olympic festival.

Two days to go

Two days before the festival began, the whole company set out from Elis, which was roughly 58 kilometres from Olympia. First came the *hellanodikai* and other officials, and then the athletes and their trainers, horses and chariots, together with their owners, jockeys and charioteers. They followed the Sacred Way along the coast, stopping to sacrifice a pig and to perform other rites at the fountain of Piera on the boundary between Elis and Olympia. They spent the night at Letrini and the next day wound their way along the valley of the Alpheios towards the Altis. The effect of such a journey on the athletes, especially those not used to long-distance walking, must have been debilitating in some cases: it is hard to see how walking the distance of a marathon on each of two consecutive days prior to the competition would have helped the boys who had to compete on the following day.

The scene is set

Meanwhile people from all walks of life had been making their way to Olympia. Princes and tyrants from Sicily and southern Italy sailed up the river in splendid barges, and ambassadors came from various towns, vying with each other in dress and paraphernalia. The rich came on horseback and in chariots; the poor came on donkeys, in carts and even on foot. Food-sellers came loaded with supplies, for there was no town near Olympia. Merchants flocked in with their wares. Artisans came to make figurines that pilgrims could buy to offer to their god. Booths and stalls were set up; tents and huts were erected, for only official delegates were given accommodation in the magnificent guest-house known as the Leonidaion. Most visitors looked for a suitable spot to put down their belongings and slept each night under the summer skies. The crowds were so great that by sunrise on the first day of the Games there was probably not a single space left from which to see the events.

5 THE PROGRAMME

Day One

Morning Swearing-in ceremony for competitors and judges in the Bouleuterion (Council House) before the altar and statue of Zeus Horkios (Zeus of the Oaths).
Contests for heralds and trumpeters held near the stadium entrance.
Boys' running, wrestling and boxing contests.
Public and private prayers and sacrifices in the Altis; consultation of oracles.
Afternoon Orations by well-known philosophers and recitals by poets and historians, perhaps also as part of competitions.
(Sightseeing tours of the Altis. Reunions with old friends.)

Day Two

Morning Procession into the hippodrome of all those competing there.
Chariot- and horse-races.
Afternoon The pentathlon: discus, javelin, jumping, running and wrestling.
Evening Funeral rites in honour of the hero Pelops.
Parade of victors round the Altis.
Communal singing of victory hymns.
Feasting and revelry.

Day Three

Morning Procession of the *hellanodikai* (judges), ambassadors from the Greek states, competitors in all events and sacrificial animals round the Altis to the Great Altar in front of the Temple of Zeus, followed by the official sacrifice of one hundred oxen given by the people of Elis.
Afternoon Foot-races.
Evening Public banquet in the Prytaneion.

Day Four

Morning Wrestling.
Midday Boxing and the *pankration* (type of all-in wrestling).
Afternoon Race-in-armour.

Day Five

Procession of victors to the Temple of Zeus where they are crowned with wreaths of wild olive by the *hellanodikai*, followed by the *phyllobolia* (when the victors are showered with leaves).
Feasting and celebrations.

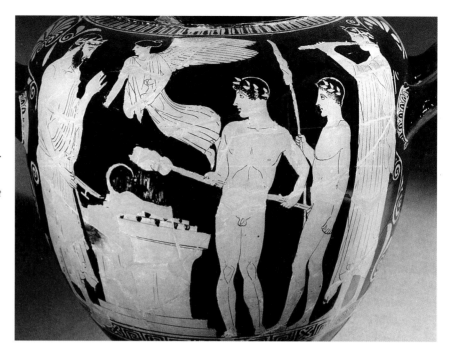

Making a thank-offering in honour of a victory. Nike, or Victory personified, flies over the altar, while a bearded man superintends the sacrifice; two athletes are ready to roast pieces of meat on spits over the fire on the altar, on which there is an ox-head. The pipe-player on the right provides music for the ceremony. Throughout the Games prayers and sacrifices were offered to Zeus and other gods. From a Greek amphora, 475–450 BC.

The above programme is hypothetical since it contains not only all the events held around 100 BC (the period represented by the model) but also, for interest, various contests which had been discontinued by that time. The order of contests at the festival is based on the surviving literary evidence but continues to be a subject of debate. When, if at all, heats for any of the events were held is uncertain. The fact that the men's running events were held on Days Three and Four suggests that heats for them may have been held on Days One and Two. The dates when the various events were introduced are listed below.

Dates for the introduction of events

Olympiad	Year BC	Event	Olympiad	Year BC	Event
I	776	Stade-race (short foot-race)	65	520	Race-in-armour
14	724	*Diaulos* (double-length foot-race)	70	500	*Apene* (mule-cart race)
15	720	*Dolichos* (long-distance foot-race)	71	496	*Calpe* or *anabates* (race for mares)
18	708	Pentathlon and wrestling	84	444	*Apene* and *calpe* discontinued
23	688	Boxing	93	408	*Synoris* (two-horse chariot-race)
25	680	*Tethrippon* (four-horse chariot-race)	96	396	Competitions for heralds and trumpeters
33	648	*Pankration* and horse-racing	99	384	Chariot-racing for teams of four colts
37	632	Foot-race and wrestling for boys	128	268	Chariot-racing for teams of two colts
38	628	Pentathlon for boys (immediately discontinued)	131	256	Races for colts
41	616	Boxing for boys	145	200	*Pankration* for boys

PUBLIC AND PRIVATE SACRIFICES

The great sacrifice to Zeus of one hundred oxen took place on the morning of the middle day of the festival, that is immediately after the full moon. The Greeks reckoned their day from sunset to sunset, so that the full moon and the sacrifice were both on the same day. After the procession had reached the Great Altar of Zeus the oxen were slaughtered, and their legs were carried to the top of the mound of ashes which had accumulated from previous sacrifices. There they were burned in honour of the god, who was believed to take sustenance from the smoke. The mortal attendants of the festival, however, took their nourishment from the rest of the ox-flesh, which was roasted later for the public banquet.

The grand procession round the Altis gave the various Greek ambassadors the opportunity to show off their wealth and finery, in particular the ceremonial vessels belonging to their city-states, which would be used for the banquet. Alkibiades, the Athenian statesman, once embarrassed his city by using the official gold and silver plate for his own private victory celebrations on the night before.

Many minor sacrifices were made throughout the festival. There were numerous altars and statues of deities in the sanctuary, and here the athletes would pray, make vows and offer thanks. Sometimes they would consult the innards of a sacrificed animal to see whether they foretold victory. The priests who resided at Olympia carried out sacrifices at sixty-nine of the altars regularly each month of every year and, furthermore, there was a programme of daily offerings or libations of wine for Zeus alone

A youth, who may be an athlete in ceremonial dress, pours a libation over flames rising from an altar. Behind the altar on a platform (shown to the right) is a herm, a pillar shaped at the top as the god Hermes, who, together with Herakles, presided over the gymnasium. Both figures wear wreaths made from long twigs. Vase made in Athens, 500–480 BC.

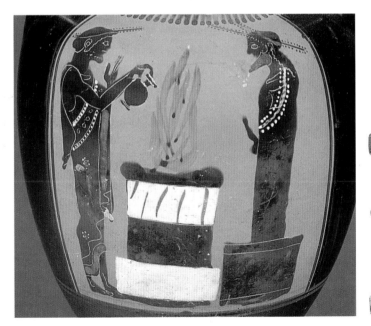

BELOW *Model of an altar, decorated with a bukranion (ox-skull) and swathes of foliage; flames twist upward from a pile of logs on top. Roman, height 7.3 cm.*

6 THE EVENTS

Charmos, a long-distance runner finished seventh in a field of six. A friend ran alongside him shouting 'Keep going, Charmos!' and although fully dressed, beat him. And if he had had five friends he would have finished twelfth.

(Nikarchos, 1st century AD, *Palatine Anthology* XI 82, after Harris)

ATHLETICS

Running

LEFT *The steady rhythm of three long-distance runners. Panathenaic amphora made in 333 BC (dated by the name of the* archon, *or chief magistrate, given on the other side); for the type of vessel, see p. 95. Height 67cm.*

It was the stade-race, or short foot-race, that determined the length of the stadium at Olympia. This was the most ancient and indeed the only event at the first thirteen Olympiads. The winner of the stade-race had the Olympiad named after him and the esteem in which he was held is indicated by the custom of dating by the list of victors. Gradually other foot-races were added to the programme at Olympia. The *diaulos*, named after the musical double pipes, consisted of two lengths of the stadium, while the *dolichos* was a long-distance race, consisting of twenty or twenty-four lengths. It was used as an opening event, no doubt because it was the longest and perhaps least spectacular race, and gave the spectators a chance to settle down.

The *dolichos*, the *diaulos* and the stade-race seem to have been features of all the major athletic festivals. The exceptional athlete who, like Polites in AD 69, won all three events at the same Olympiad, was called a *triastes,* or 'tripler'. The greatest Olympic runner of all was Leonidas of Rhodes, who, 'with the speed of a god', won all three events at each of the four successive Olympiads between 164 and 152 BC. For a runner to maintain such a peak of fitness (all the running events were held on the same day) for twelve years was a remarkable feat, and such was

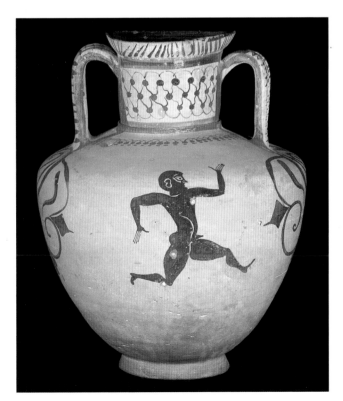

The vigorous action of a sprinter. Amphora made in eastern Greece, c.550–525 BC. Height 34.2 cm.

the pride of his countrymen that he became worshipped as a local deity. But the very fact that athletes did occasionally win all three events suggests that standards and depth of competition were, in comparison with modern times, relatively low. It would be unthinkable for a single athlete nowadays to win both the 200 metres and the 5,000 metres (the nearest modern equivalent to the *dolichos*). The ancient results are more comparable to those of the early modern Olympics: in the 1896 Olympics the same man won both the 100 metres and the 1,200 metres in the swimming events, and in the cycling events the same man won both the one-lap race and the 15-kilometre race.

There also existed at Olympia the *hoplitodromia*, or race-in-armour (a hoplite was a heavily armed foot-soldier). This was the last of the running races to be added to the programme, in 520 BC. Competitors wore a helmet and greaves (lower-leg armour) and carried a round shield, although it is possible that in later years both helmet and greaves were discarded. Twenty-five runners were allowed to take part, and a set of shields was kept in the Temple of Zeus for them. Presumably this was to ensure that each athlete carried a shield of the same weight. In some of the games contestants were decked out

Bronze greaves and Corinthian-style helmet. The armour worn by competitors in the hoplitodromia *(race-in-armour) must have proved a considerable handicap. Each of these greaves weighs about 0.64 kg and the helmet 1.46 kg. The greaves would have pulled open and clipped around the leg, and like the helmet they were probably lined with leather. About 520–480 BC, height 23 cm (helmet), 42 cm (greaves).*

A judge watches two armed runners passing a finishing post. The winner has taken off his helmet and looks round at the other competitor who has flung down his shield. The shield device may be some kind of plant. Drinking-cup made in Athens, 500–475 BC, height 9.2 cm, diameter 22.5 cm.

in armour from head to foot. A curious, clanking race, it must have had both serious and comic connotations: serious because all athletic training was devised to keep the male citizen population physically fit for war. Its position at the very end of the festival left a final reminder of this to the assembled crowds. However, amusing mishaps and collisions inevitably occurred. On scenes from pottery we often see athletes who have dropped their shields and are stooping to pick them up. The Greeks themselves must have considered it something of a diversion, since when Peisthetairos, a character in Aristophanes' *Birds*, sees the Chorus advancing in their feathered costumes, he likens the motley crew to the armed runners in the *hoplitodromia*. A modern counterpart to the *hoplitodromia* is the steeplechase: in both events running is deliberately impeded. For the Greeks part of the significance of the race in armour may have been encompassed in the saying *kala ta chalepa*: the more difficult the task, the greater glory that results from accomplishing it. Hence, perhaps, the reason why the race-in-armour was the last race in the running programme, bringing the running events to a glorious finale. Nowadays the men's 1,500 metres is the blue-ribbon climactic event.

Armed runners taking part in the hoplitodromia, *or race-in-armour, in a scene from a Panathenaic amphora. This vessel can be dated to the year 336 BC, from the name of the* archon *given on the other side.*

At other games there were various additions to the running programme. One was the *hippios* or 'horsey' race, probably referring to the fact that it was the same distance as the horse-race, i.e. six lengths of the stadium. A curtain raiser at some festivals was the *lampadedromia*, a relay race with a torch as a baton, contested by teams of six to ten in which the winner was the first to arrive home with his torch still alight. As a reward he was granted the honour of lighting the fire on the sacrificial altar. The modern

Olympics have borrowed the idea of this event as a means of starting the Games, with a relay of runners carrying the Olympic flame from Olympia to the Games venue, but it was definitely not part of the ancient Olympic festival.

There is one foot-race that has not been mentioned so far and that is the marathon, which is an entirely modern event. It is true that, according to Greek tradition, some ancient runners were able to cover amazing distances. The most famous is the original 'marathon runner' Pheidippides, who covered 260 kilometres of rugged terrain in less than two days. When in 490 BC the Athenians learned that the Persians had landed at Marathon *en route* to attack Athens, he ran to Sparta with a request for help – a feat commemorated nowadays in the Spartathlon race from Athens to Sparta, fittingly won a number of times in recent years by the incredible Greek ultra-distance runner, Ioannis Kouros, whose best time for the distance is less than 24 hours. Another remarkable achievement occurred in the fourth century BC when Drymos ran all the way from Elis to Epidauros to announce his own Olympic victory, a journey via the mountains of Arcadia of over 130 kilometres. But the concept of any cross-country event at an athletic festival was totally alien to ancient Greek sport, as it still is in the modern Olympics.

A starting sill in the stadium at Olympia, with grooves for the runner's toes. In the foreground is one of the basins that provided water for the spectators.

'They're off!'

Like modern athletes, before taking their places at the starting line, the runners did a few warming-up exercises, which the Roman poet Statius describes as running on the spot, dropping on to the haunches, beating the chest, sprinting forward and coming to an abrupt halt. Then they stood restless and impatient, ready for the crucial test. Often a great many contestants would enter for the races, and earlier in the day the runners would draw lots from a bronze bowl or helmet to settle the heats, so that only the very best would be pitted against one another in the final.

For the sprint events the starting position was quite different from that used today. An ancient athlete did not crouch down like his modern counterpart; instead he used a standing start with arms stretched forward, one foot slightly in front of the other, left or right according to preference, and toes firmly gripping the grooves in the marble sill comparable to the way modern athletes start middle-distance events.

ABOVE *A runner, poised to take off in the customary upright starting position, is depicted on a miniature* lekythos, *or oil-jar, which was either a toy or an offering. Perspective on Greek vases is a matter of convention rather than accuracy, for in reality the runner stood beside the post with his toes gripping the grooves in the sill. Made in Athens about 450–425 BC, height 11 cm.*

ABOVE RIGHT *Bronze statuette of a trumpeter from southern Italy. Competitions for trumpeters and heralds were held in the Echo Colonnade (p. 26) on the first day of the festival. The winners signalled the start and announced the results of the other competitions. About 470 BC (the trumpet may be modern), height 14.6 cm.*

The signal for the off was given either by the herald's trumpet or by the shout *apite*, 'Go!'. Those who jumped the start suffered the severe punishment of being flogged by the policeman known as the *alytes*. In races of more than one length the greatest burst of speed would be in the first stretch in order to get clear of the turning post, and this, as in the hippodrome, was the likeliest place for collisions, fouls and cheating, including taking a short cut without rounding the post, which was only too tempting amid a throng of runners.

In some of the surviving scenes the post seems to have been fitted with a large base to minimize the risk of the runners grabbing hold of it to swing themselves round, which would be a natural impulse. Other familiar faults were holding, tripping or running in front of an opponent.

Just as today, styles of running varied according to the race. The postures of figures on the vases are not always entirely accurate since artists relied heavily on conventional poses, but nevertheless they are an informative guide. Sprinters display the most vigour, arms and legs darting furiously to and fro in a flat-out dash down the track. The *dolichos* runner, on the other hand, reserved his energy by keeping his arms bent up close to his sides, and swinging them in relatively relaxed fashion. Only on the final lap did he suddenly spurt toward the finishing post making violent arm movements like the sprinter. Presumably the technique of the *diaulos* runner was somewhere midway between the two. In remarking on the physical requirements of the two types of runner, Philostratus recommends that the long-distance man should have slender legs and strength in the neck and shoulders, since he needed to swing his arms for a much greater distance (see illustrations pp. 56-7).

Nearly all the scenes depicted on pottery show athletes competing nude. Both Homer and Thucydides, however, record that in earlier times athletes wore a type of loin-cloth, though in both cases interpretation is controversial. Two reasons were given for the discontinuation of this garb. One is that a runner competing at Athens was in the lead when unfortunately his shorts came adrift, and he tripped and fell over them. The *archon* Hippomenes then passed a law that, to avoid future accidents of this nature, all athletes were to perform naked. According to the second version, Orrhippos or Orsippos of Megara won the stade-race at Olympia in 720 BC, but lost his shorts in the process and thus set a new trend. A more likely reason is that Greek men were always proud of their muscular, sun-tanned bodies, and were only too eager to contrast their excellent physical condition with that of barbarians who preferred to keep themselves covered up. We know that runners, like other sportsmen, liberally oiled their skin before an event. The poet Bacchylides tells how Aglaos of Athens rushed into the cheering crowds at the end of a race and bespattered the spectators' garments with oil.

At the end of each contest the names of the victor, his father and his city-state were proclaimed by the herald. Most important of all was the winner of the stade-race, for, as he had won the most hallowed of all races, the Olympiad was named after him.

The pentathlon

The pentathlon was a test for the all-round athlete. The five events (which are discussed individually below) were discus, jumping, javelin, running and wrestling, held in that order during the course of one afternoon. The last two events existed as competitions in their own right but the other three were not found outside the pentathlon. It is not clear just how the winner of the pentathlon was decided, but it seems likely that, if an athlete won the first three events, he would be declared the overall winner, and the running and wrestling competitions would be cancelled.

The pentathlete's skill lay in versatility, and the contest was probably invented to discover the athlete who possessed this quality. The pentathlete's physical appearance was much admired, for the variety of exertion gave him a particularly supple body, which lacked what the Greeks considered to be unsightly, overdeveloped muscles. Aristotle praises his fleetness of foot and strength of build.

For all its moderation the pentathlon was certainly not an undemanding contest. In particular it required great powers of endurance. This is confirmed by the fact that, when the boys' pentathlon was introduced at Olympia in 628 BC, it was immediately discontinued, presumably because it was too exacting and not, as Pausanias would have us believe, because a Spartan won it.

Discus-throwing

Phlegyas of Pisa...first roughens the discus and his own hand with earth; then shaking off the dust he turns it dexterously to see which side best suits his fingers, or fits more snugly the middle of his arm. He had always loved this sport, and used to practise throwing the discus across the Alpheios where the banks are furthest apart, always clearing the river and never getting the discus wet...

(Statius, 1st century AD, *Thebaid* VI 670–77)

Bronze discus, which was thrown by Exoidas when he won a contest in Kephallenia. He dedicated the discus to Castor and Pollux, the twin sons of Zeus; Castor was renowned as a discus-thrower. The spiral inscription is written retrograde (right to left) in archaic Greek lettering. 6th century BC, diameter 16.5 cm, weight 1.25 kg.

Discus-throwing is a curious sport. Today hardly anyone would question the choice of a circular, flat object as a throwing weight because we appreciate the aerodynamic qualities of this shape. The Greeks, although not aware of the technicalities, presumably realized that the thin, round, water-smoothed pebbles that they found in river-beds could be thrown further and faster than simple stones. Despite this knowledge, the throwing of large spherical stones, *lithobolos*, existed in several places as a contest in its own right. Normally the stones would have weighed no more than a few kilograms, but a record stone-throw was claimed by a man called Bubon, for in the museum at Olympia there is a boulder which bears this inscription: 'Bubon...the son of Pholos, threw me over his head with one hand.' The boulder weighs 143.5 kg, nearly 316 lb, so the feat was almost certainly impossible.

Although stone-throwing bears some similarities to modern shot-putting it was not included in the ancient Olympic Games, whereas discus-throwing was. Apart from its aerodynamic shape, there was an additional reason for the adoption of the discus. In the *Iliad* Homer describes the funeral games held

in honour of Patroklos before the walls of Troy. Achilles offered a valuable ingot of iron, which was then a precious metal, to the man who could throw it farthest. We know from surviving examples that such ingots were similar in shape to the discus; this was because the metal was poured into open, circular moulds scooped out in the sand, forming ingots curved on one side and flat on the other. The suitability of the object as a throwing weight must have been obvious. Although ingots may have been used in competitions for some years, they were eventually replaced by the purpose-made discus. The discus itself was no longer the prize in the competition: it was merely a piece of equipment.

About twenty ancient discuses have survived; most are bronze, a few are marble, and one is lead. They vary in diameter from about 17 to 35 cm, with an average thickness of 0.5 cm. The weights range from approximately 1.5 to 6.5 kg, 2.5 kg being the average, just 0.5 kg more than the minimum weight for a modern discus, which is usually made of wood, with an inner metal plate and rim.

The discrepancies in the weights and measurements of the ancient discuses are not so surprising when we consider that they were not all necessarily intended for actual use; some may have been made expressly as religious offerings. Varying local standards of weight must also be taken into account, plus the fact that discuses of different weights were used for the men's and boys' events. This distinction is implied by Pausanias, who records that some colossal bones, thought to be those of Ajax, were found on Salamis, the knee-cap being 'as big as a boy's discus'.

At Olympia three 'official' discuses were kept in the Treasury of the Sikyonians; these would have been used in competitions to ensure fairness. An amusing legend suggests that the Olympic discus was particularly heavy. According to the legend, the ghost of Protesilaos, the first Greek to be killed in the Trojan War, was 4.6 metres (15 feet) tall and haunted a vineyard near Gallipoli; being a kindly soul, he would help the local farmer, but in his spare time this awesome spectre practised athletics, throwing a discus 'twice the weight of the one used at Olympia'.

There has been a great deal of discussion about the method of discus-throwing used in antiquity. Paintings and sculptures usually depict the discus-thrower in one of several conventional poses, so that it is difficult to reconstruct the whole series of movements. No doubt athletes had their own individual styles just as they do now, but the series of drawings on p. 66 illustrates what seems to be the commonest method. There is no evidence that the athlete made more than a three-quarter turn before throwing the discus, whereas today the thrower will spin round two and a half times to give impulsion.

Very little is known about the length of the throws achieved in antiquity, and those that are recorded are something of a surprise. One was made in about 480 BC by Phaullos, a somewhat legendary figure who fought in the

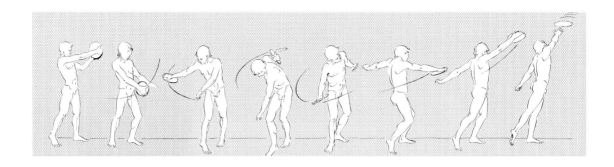

An attempt to reconstruct the ancient method of discus-throwing.

Battle of Salamis and was also a renowned athlete. He won two victories in the pentathlon and one in the foot-race at Delphi, where a statue was erected to record his achievements. Phaullos made the only discus throw to be recorded in an epigram, and it is therefore likely to have been a remarkable feat. The throw measured a mere 30 metres. The current Olympic record is 67.5 metres and, as discus-throwing had already been practised for centuries before Phaullos' time, by today's standards this was certainly not a medal-winning performance. The length of the other recorded throw was one of 45.7 metres by the amiable ghost whom we met earlier, which can hardly count, but one would perhaps expect something apparently phenomenal from this superhuman athlete. A possible explanation is that the accepted method of throwing was so stylized as to prevent the athlete from using his full potential for distance. To the Greeks rhythm and grace were of vital importance in athletics; it is known that exercise was often performed to the accompaniment of music and it is more than likely that the discus-thrower attempted to achieve almost a dance movement. The centrifugal force employed in today's free-style discus-throwing has undoubtedly made possible a dramatic increase in length of throw.

Javelin-throwing

We recommend two Persian javelins of cornel wood… and we advise throwing the javelin from as great a distance as possible, for this gives a man more time to turn his horse and to grasp the other javelin. Here are some brief instructions on the most effective method of throwing a javelin. If a man draws back his right side as he advances with the left, rises a little from the thighs and discharges the javelin with its point a little upwards, he will give his weapon the strongest impetus and the furthest carrying power…

(Xenophon, 4th century BC, *On the Art of Horsemanship* XII *12–13*)

Javelin-throwing, of all athletic events, had the strongest connections with warfare. From Mycenaean times until the Roman Empire, soldiers relied heavily upon the javelin as an offensive weapon. It differed from the spear in that it was lighter and was thrown rather than thrust. It enabled a man to attack the enemy from a distance before engaging in hand-to-hand fighting,

The method of holding a javelin by the thong as used by the javelin-thrower on the left in the picture above. Sometimes the thong was knotted onto the shaft, while on others it was merely twisted round and came free after the throw.

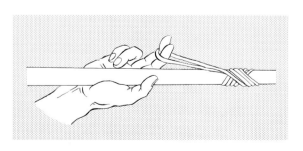

and was particularly effective when thrown from horseback, as Xenophon demonstrated. At some games mounted javelin-throwing at a target was included in the programme, but at Olympia contestants competed on foot.

Athletes used javelins which were lighter than the military ones, for their object was distance rather than penetration. These athletic javelins were made of elderwood, while soldiers used a type made from a hardwood like cornel or yew. The athletic javelin was roughly the height of the thrower and it seems that for practice purposes it was often blunt. In a competition the point would probably be sharpened, so that it would stick into the ground, otherwise it would have been difficult to measure the length of the throw.

There was one major difference between the ancient and the modern technique of throwing a javelin: Greek athletes used a leather thong (*ankyle*) which was wound round the middle of the shaft. When the javelin was thrown, the thong unwound, having the same effect as the spiral grooves inside a rifle barrel: it made the javelin spin, ensuring a steadier flight. Modern experiments have shown that use of the thong increases the chances of pitching on the point, although it has hardly any effect on distance. We have no detailed information about the length of the throws that were achieved in ancient times, since in general there seems to have been little concern about making records, but contemporary writers imply that throws of 91 metres were possible.

Except for the use of the thong the Greek method of javelin-throwing was identical to

ours. The athlete ran up to the mark carrying the javelin in his right hand horizontally at ear-level, brought it back for the throw extending his left arm forward to aid his balance, and then thrust the javelin forward. The contest took place in the stadium and competitors were required to throw from the same *balbis* (rectangular area) as the discus-throwers used. They were probably allowed three throws, as athletes depicted on pottery often carry three javelins, and at games on the island of Kos victors were given three javelins as a prize.

Long-jump

Student: Just now Sokrates asked Chairophon how many of its own feet a flea could jump – do you see? – because one of them had just bitten Chairophon's eyebrow and jumped over onto Sokrates' head.

Strepsiades: Well, how did he find out?

Student: He used a most elegant method. He melted some wax and then dipped the flea's feet into it, so that when it was set the flea had a pair of Persian slippers on. And then he took them off its feet and measured the distance out, like this, you see… (taking a step or two, toe touching heel)

(Aristophanes, 5th century BC, *Clouds* 142–50)

Aristophanes' audience would often have seen athletes pacing out the length of their jumps to see how well they had done. The flea could not be expected to follow suit and so the obvious solution was to find out his shoe size and use it as a unit of measure.

The long-jump was the only type of jumping contest in Greek athletics. It must be remembered that every event was originally intended as a form of training for warfare, and the long-jump might have been useful for crossing obstacles like a ravine or stream. The high-jump might also have proved helpful, but perhaps it was ignored because it needs more skill than strength and requires special apparatus and a soft landing. In ancient depictions the only time that we see someone using a pole in the same manner as the modern pole-vaulter is to leap on to a horse, although Homer tells us that the agile Nestor once escaped the charge of the Calydonian Boar by pole-vaulting into a tree with the aid of his hunting-spear.

One glance at a representation of a Greek long-jumper will show the vital difference between the ancient and modern methods. The Greeks always used weights called *halteres*. On take-off they were swung forward with as much force as possible, propelling the jumper forward. As he came down to land he

The probable way in which jumping weights were used.

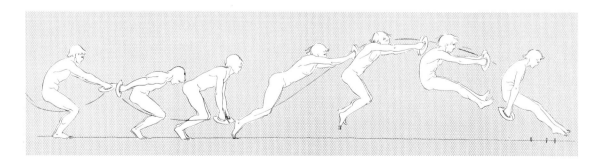

swung them backwards, providing the thrust to achieve those vital extra inches. Philostratus says that the jumper was disqualified unless he made a clean impression in the sand with both feet: modern athletes experimenting with weights have found, however, that the only way to obtain a clean landing is to cast them away over the shoulders on descent. If they were retained, the jumper tended to sit backwards in the sand, and if they were thrown away underarm, he tipped forward. No doubt the ancient athlete acquired his skill from constant practice. Even the Greeks regarded it as the most difficult of events, and Philostratus says that is the reason why the pipes were so often played to accompany the jump. Just like today, music was often played to accompany exercise – aerobics would almost seem impossible without it! To achieve an outstanding jump, split-second timing was essential in the movement of arms and legs. The value of the music in creating rhythm and encouraging concentration was thought to be more necessary here than in any other contest.

Though we are used to seeing a running start, it is not certain that this method was used in antiquity. The sill in the stadium, which served as a take-off point (*bater*), was only 18.3 metres from the perimeter. This would not allow enough space for the modern method. The recent trials mentioned above also indicated that the weights were unwieldy in a running leap and that they reduced the length of the jump which was otherwise possible. But again, is it a question of practice? It seems quite possible, to judge from surviving illustrations, that a short run was used, that the jumper started with the weights held close up to his body, ran a short way still holding them to the front, then as he neared the take-off point he swung them back at arm's length and then forward on the moment of take-off. Another possibility is that weights were used not to facilitate the jump at all but to deliberately make the event harder and more physically demanding, just as nowadays hurdles provide an extra difficulty in sprint events.

A number of *halteres* have survived. Like the discuses they vary in size and weight. The lengths are between 12 and 29 cm, and the weights between about 1 and 4.5 kg. They also differ in shape and it is possible to date the periods when each type was most popular. The earliest ones, in use by the middle of the sixth century BC, are similar in shape to the handset of an old-fashioned telephone and made of either stone or metal. Towards the end of the century they were modified: the front end became heavier, and size

BELOW *A pair of flat jumping weights made out of lead, weighing 1.07 kg each (undamaged). 5th century* BC, *length 19 cm.*

BOTTOM *Cylindrical stone jumping weight (2.23 kg) with carved finger grips. Height 20.3 cm.*

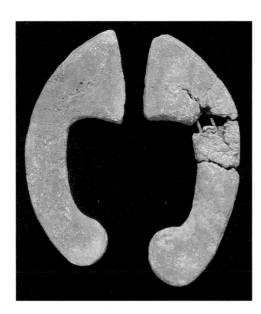

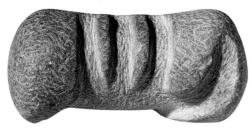

and position of the recess for the thumb and fingers indicate that it must have been held further towards the back. The lead and iron examples are usually flat. During the fifth century BC another type was introduced which was usually made of stone in the shape of a bar, flat underneath, rounded on top and rounded or pointed at each end. It was held by means of recesses carved out in the sides. After the fifth century it is not certain which sort of *halter* was preferred, but Roman copies of Greek statues of jumpers usually show a cylindrical type with hemispherical ends and grooves for the fingers.

For us the greatest problem about the ancient long-jump is in determining whether it was a single, double or even triple jump. Only two measurements of ancient jumps are now recorded. One was in about 480 BC by Phaullos of Croton, whom we met earlier as a discus-thrower, and this was 16.3 metres. The other was by Chionis of Sparta who, around the middle of the century, achieved a jump of 16.7 metres. Both these are almost double the current record of 8.95 metres for a single jump, and therefore they have often been rejected as pure fiction on the grounds of sheer physical impossibility. But they do make sense if we assume that the ancient event was some kind of multiple jump. (The current triple-jump record is 18.29 metres.) This appears to be confirmed by a statement in Aristotle's *Physics*, where he says that the jump in the pentathlon is not a single continuous movement (though he could be referring to the discontinuous movement required to swing arms and legs back and forth). Further, Phaullos' noteworthy jump apparently rewarded him with a broken leg since he landed on hard ground, 1.5 metres beyond the end of the *skamma*, or sandpit. It would have been scarcely necessary to maintain a 15.2-metre pit for jumps which were normally only about one-third of this length, unless of course the pit was used for jumping from either end.

COMBAT

The 'heavy' events as the Greeks called them – wrestling, the *pankration* (a kind of all-in wrestling) and boxing – were always big attractions at the Games. But they were more than mere sport and entertainment, they were one of the essential aspects of Greek athletic education. Experience in the martial arts was of paramount importance to the future warrior. Wealthy families could afford to hire a trainer, a *paidotribes*, who is frequently depicted on pottery and sealstones instructing his pupils with the aid of a cleft stick. With professional tuition unarmed combat became almost an art. Those who could not afford to exercise in the *palaistra* with a private trainer practised in the public gymnasium. The Spartans, however, rejected the 'niceties' taught by a professional tutor, and chose instead to rely on sheer power and endurance. One young Spartan composed a boastful epigram on this theme: 'The other wrestlers are stylists. I win by my strength, as is only right and fitting for a Spartan youth.'

Wrestling

You, throw your arms around him – You, get under his grip. You, push your foot between his and close with him…

(From a 2nd-century-AD papyrus giving instructions for wrestling drill)

The end of a contest in the pankration. *The victor aims a final blow, while the loser raises his right index finger in submission. The man on the right makes sure that the judge has noticed. Greek amphora, c.520–500 BC.*

There were basically two types of wrestling: upright or proper wrestling, and ground wrestling. The distinction was in the types of hold that were allowed and the method of deciding the victor. In the first the object was to throw the opponent to the ground. Three falls were necessary to win, and hence the victor became known as the *triakter*, or 'trebler'. Touching the ground with the back, shoulders or hip constituted a fall. The contest continued without intervals until one man had thrown his opponent three times. In ground wrestling victory did not depend on the number of falls but continued until one competitor acknowledged defeat. This was done by raising the right hand with the index finger pointed.

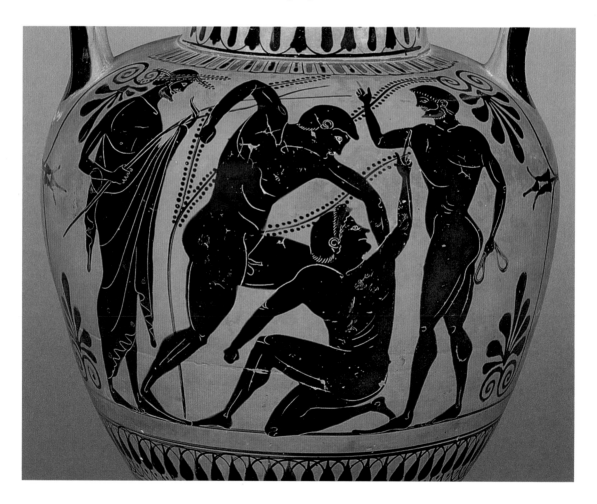

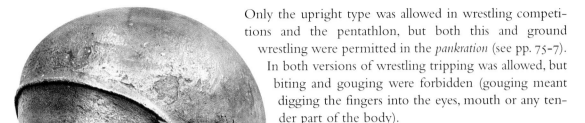

Only the upright type was allowed in wrestling competitions and the pentathlon, but both this and ground wrestling were permitted in the *pankration* (see pp. 75-7). In both versions of wrestling tripping was allowed, but biting and gouging were forbidden (gouging meant digging the fingers into the eyes, mouth or any tender part of the body).

Both sports were allotted their own specific area within the *palaistra*: upright wrestling usually took place in the *skamma*, a carefully levelled and sanded section of ground, while ground-wrestling was often staged in an area specially watered to make it muddy and sticky, so that it became known as the *keroma*, or 'beeswax'.

Like other athletes, wrestlers anointed themselves with olive oil. Powder was then dusted on to afford the opponent a grip, otherwise it would have been rather like the old game of 'catch the greasy pig'. Aristophanes, however, relates how unscrupulous wrestlers would secretly wipe an oily hand over some part of their body that the opponent was likely to grasp. He also tells of a wrestler who was thrown and then hastily rubbed off the sand from his shoulders to remove the evidence of a fall. Wrestlers, like other sportsmen, competed nude and wore their hair short so that it could not be grasped by their opponent. Some wore a tight-fitting leather cap, like one that the Roman poet Martial sent to a friend 'so that the duty of the mud-ring may not soil your sleek hair'.

The head of a wrestler wearing a leather cap to prevent his opponent from gripping his hair. Etruscan, 3rd century BC, height 20.3 cm.

It seems that up to sixteen competitors took part in a contest; two sets of lots, both marked with the letters of the alphabet, were drawn from a helmet or bronze bowl, and the two wrestlers who drew the same letter were required to fight each other. If there was an odd number of contestants, one man drew a bye, as in boxing (see p. 79). If there was only one entrant, he would win without having to fight, and if so he was said to win *akonitei*, 'without touching the dust'. On one occasion this happened to Milo, a wrestler from Croton in southern Italy, who lived in the sixth century BC. On his way to receive the crown he had the misfortune to slip and fall on his hip; the crowd jested that he should not win after having had a 'fall'.

Most of our evidence for the holds and tackles employed in Greek wrestling comes from the scenes on pottery, portraying not only real life but also mythological contests between gods, heroes and beasts. The artists could find inspiration for these scenes in their local *palaistra* or gymnasium.

The illustrations on pp. 74–7 show a variety of tactics. There was no weight distinction in any of the contests and consequently the biggest men tended to win, although Aristotle warned against over-feeding and also over-training boy athletes. He believed that it made them muscle-bound and lethargic. It seems that few boy athletes went on to win in adult competitions for, of all

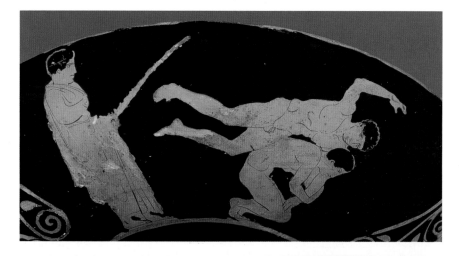

the boy victors recorded at Olympia, only two won victories in the contests for men.

The greatest wrestler of all time was probably Milo from Croton in southern Italy, mentioned earlier. He won five times at Olympia and gained another twenty-five victories at other 'circuit' games. Only when attempting a sixth Olympic victory, when he must have been at least thirty-nine or forty years old, was he finally defeated by a younger man, Timotheos. Milo's popularity, however, was undiminished, and the crowd rushed into the stadium, lifted him onto their shoulders and carried him round, Timotheos cheering along with them.

Many tales were told about Milo. Once he is said to have eaten a whole four-year-old heifer which, earlier the same day, he had carried all round the Altis. On another occasion, during the sampling of the new wine at the *anthesterion* festival, he downed three *choai* (about 9 litres) of wine, all for a bet. This amazing character was also reputed to be a disciple of Pythagoras and to have written several treatises. His end was both tragic and ironic. While out in the forest one day he came upon a newly cut tree trunk with the wedges in place ready for it to be split open. He decided to use his own strength to force it apart. The wedges flew out, but his hands were trapped, and that night he was eaten by wild animals. The story, perhaps apocryphal (a similar story is told of the pankratiast Polydamas of Skotussa), illustrates that the presence of brawn does not necessarily imply the presence of brain.

In the struggle between two pankratiasts on the ground the man on the right tries to gouge out his opponent's eye, a foul for which the trainer is about to strike him with his cleft stick. Behind hang a bundle of boxing thongs and a discus in a bag, and on the left are two boxers. From a Greek drinking-cup, c.500–475 BC.

Pankration

Pankratiasts…must employ backward falls which are not safe for the wrestler… They must have skill in various methods of strangling; they also wrestle with an opponent's ankle and twist his arm, besides hitting and jumping on him, for all these practices belong to the pankration, only biting and gouging being excepted.

(Philostratus, 2nd–3rd century AD, *On Gymnastics*)

It is no surprise that at least one athlete, Sarapion of Alexandria, ran away the day before the *pankration* because he was afraid of his opponents. The *pankration* may seem the most violent of Greek sports to us; the Greeks, however, considered it less dangerous than boxing. Because it was such a crowd-puller, it was one of the first sports to be taken over by professionals. By the end of the fourth century BC few amateurs entered the contests and at many of the local games the prize-money for the *pankration* was considerably more than for any other event. Prizes were given not merely for brute strength: skill was

Herakles executes a ladder-grip on Triton, who was half-man, half-fish. Artists adapted scenes that they saw in the palaistra *and* gymnasium *for mythological battles. From a Greek amphora, c.520–500 BC.*

Bronze coin of Antoninus Pius (AD 138-61), from Alexandria, showing Herakles using a body-lift on the giant Antaios.

just as essential as it was in wrestling. Eight of Pindar's Odes are in honour of pankratiasts, and they refer to all the qualities that symbolized the contemporary athletic ideal.

Both upright and ground wrestling, which have already been described, were allowed in the *pankration*. Striking with the fist or open hand was also allowed, and leg- and foot-holds were common. As in ground wrestling, the object was to force your opponent to submit, and although gouging and biting were forbidden, scenes on pottery show that pankratiasts often tried to get away with both. Biting was certainly ridiculed, and Plutarch tells how Alkibiades, as a desperate measure to avoid being thrown, bit his opponent's hand; the other released his grip, exclaiming, 'You bite, like a woman, Alkibiades.' 'No,' he answered, 'like a lion.' Kicking was also scorned, and in his parody of the Olympic Games Galen, a Roman physician of the second century AD, awards the prize for the *pankration* to the donkey since it was the best of all animals at kicking.

At the beginning of a bout contestants usually sparred with their hands and fists, twisting each other's arms and fingers; this was known as *akrocheirismos*. Sostratos, a pankratiast from Sikyon, was famous for breaking his opponent's fingers to gain a submission at the very beginning of the contest. Because of this habit he became known as 'Mr Finger-Tips'. Pausanias disapproved of this trick and says that it was used only by contestants who could not achieve a fall. Most of the struggle took place on the ground, as each of the combatants wished to avoid a heavy fall, and learning to 'wrestle on the knees' was one aspect of a thorough training.

Pankratiasts from different regions had their own specialities. One short cut to victory was the stranglehold, which was greatly favoured by the Eleans, but the ladder-grip, *klimakismos*, was most effective, as admirably demonstrated by Herakles and the Triton (shown above). Lucian's *Anacharsis* humorously describes how the enemies of the Greeks would take flight for fear of this hold, 'lest as they stand gaping, you fill their mouths with sand, or jumping round to get on their backs, twist your legs round their bellies, squeeze your arms beneath their helmets, and strangle them to death'.

A spectacular feat was the stomach-throw, where a man grabbed hold of his opponent, rolled on to his back and, planting his foot firmly in the other's stomach, propelled him clean over his head to a thunderous landing, as in the judo throw *tomonagi*. Referring to such tactics, Pindar likens Melissos to the

Two wrestlers at the moment before the would-be victor dashes the upended man to the ground; the latter thrusts down his arm to lessen the impact. From a bronze statuette, early 2nd century BC, height 25 cm.

fox that rolls on her back 'spreads out her feet and deflects the swoop of the eagle'.

As leg- and foot-holds were permitted in the *pankration*, a man would often grasp his opponent by the foot, lift it up and tilt him over backwards. A small stocky Cilician athlete, nicknamed 'Jumping Weight', because he was shaped like one, won great renown for his 'heel-trick'. Instead of releasing his opponent's foot after obtaining a fall in this way, he would keep hold of it, forcing a submission by twisting it out of its socket.

The most famous Olympic pankratiasts were Theagenes of Thasos and Polydamas of Skotussa. Theagenes won 1,400 crowns at various Greek festivals and his strength was reputedly so great that at the age of nine he picked up a bronze statue he took a fancy to in the local market-place and carried it off. In subsequent years his own statue stood at Olympia next to that of Alexander the Great. Amongst other achievements, Polydamas was said to have strangled a lion with his bare hands, a feat that is depicted on his statue-base, which survives at Olympia. He is also credited with having stopped a chariot dead in its tracks by seizing hold of it as it sped past him.

Boxing

Glaukos was originally a farmer. One day the ploughshare came away from the plough and his father observed Glaukos hammering it back with his bare fist. Impressed by his son's great strength, the old man decided to take him to the next Olympic Games. This he did and Glaukos fought his way through to the final of the contest. But he was inexperienced and so took a great deal of punishment in the preliminary bouts. Consequently when he came to face his last opponent he was so badly wounded that everybody thought he would have to give up, but his father called out to him 'My boy, remember the ploughshare!', whereupon Glaukos hit his opponent so hard that the contest was ended there and then.

(Pausanias, 2nd century AD, *Description of Greece* VI 10, 1–3)

Boxing is a very ancient sport, depicted by artists as early as the Minoan and Mycenaean periods. The Greeks always liked to embellish time-honoured tradition with divine origins. The god Apollo, who was particularly associated with boxing, is said to have beaten Ares, god of war, in the first-ever boxing contest at Olympia. Herakles

Seated boxer wearing caestus *(see p. 80) with fleece around the forearms for mopping up sweat. His scarred and battered face, broken nose and cauliflower ear show that he is a seasoned fighter, and his weary appearance suggests that he has recently fought in a long contest. From a bronze statue, 3rd–2nd century BC, height 1.2 metres.*

was also renowned for his boxing skills, but it was the legendary hero Theseus who was credited with its invention, under the guidance of Athena.

More realistically, the origins of boxing were attributed to the Spartans. In early times they were said to have fought without helmets, considering a shield the only manly form of protection. Boxing hardened their faces and taught them to ward off blows to the head. Ironically, they usually refrained from taking part in public boxing contests and the *pankration*. These contests were decided when a competitor was either knocked insensible or admitted defeat, which would have brought dishonour to a Spartan.

A slim athlete stands ready to wrestle, although his corpulent companion, boxing thongs in hand, would clearly prefer fisticuffs. Philostratus says that a paunch was a useful asset to a boxer because it made it more difficult for his opponent to score a blow to the head. From a Greek drinking-cup, c.510–500 BC.

Two boxers on a fragment of a Mycenaean pot from Cyprus, c.1300–1200 BC, height 19.6 cm.

Boxing was especially popular in the east, and during the early years of the Olympic festival most of the champions were Ionian Greeks from Asia Minor and the islands off its coast. Onomastos of Smyrna, victor of Olympia in 688 BC, is said to have formulated the rules for boxing which were adopted at the Olympic Games, and this, comments Philostratus, was 'although he came from effeminate Ionia'. The eastern Greeks were often scorned for being somewhat flabby but in boxing this may have amounted to an asset rather than a liability.

The precise nature of the rules can only be the subject of conjecture, based on the surviving illustrations and literacy references. It seems that no wrestling or holding was allowed, but it was permissible to hit a fallen man. Virtually any type of blow with the hand was allowed, but gouging with the thumb was forbidden. Scenes on pottery show the use of the hook, upper cuts and rabbit punches, and blows with the side and heel of the hand were not uncommon.

Contests often lasted for many hours, and sometimes the boxers agreed to exchange undefended blows in order to end the contest before nightfall. A fight at Nemea between Damoxenos and Kreugas ended in this way, and it exemplifies the violence of ancient boxing. Kreugas struck first with a blow to his opponent's head; Damoxenos rallied, and jabbed Kreugas under the ribs with outstretched fingers so viciously that the blow pierced his flesh and tore out the entrails; Kreugas died instantly. It is often claimed that boxing became more bloodthirsty in Roman times, but this brutality would be hard to equal. There are surprisingly few references to fatal accidents in boxing during the one thousand sand years that contests were held. On such occasions the dead man was posthumously awarded the crown and his opponent banished forever from the stadium where the contests were held.

The fights did not take place in a ring, which meant that there was no opportunity for cornering, and at Olympia the boxing events were at midday, so that neither competitor had the sun in his eyes. As in other combat events, lots were drawn beforehand, and if there was an odd number of contestants one man drew a bye, which meant that for the next heat he became an *ephedros*, or 'sitter-by'. At the start of the contest, boxers advanced *deinon derkomenoi*, 'with looks that could kill'; there was no bonhomie or shaking of hands.

It is difficult to trace the evolution of the sport, but the development of the glove reflects some of the changes that took place. Until around 500 BC the 'well-cut thongs of ox-hide' recorded by Homer remained standard. These thin strips of leather 3–3.7 metres long are often depicted hanging in bundles in the *palaistra*. They were secured to the hand by a loop at each end, and we often see athletes adjusting them before the contest. The thongs were occasionally dressed with oil or fat to keep them supple; although they were known as 'soft' gloves, their purpose was probably to protect the knuckles rather than to avoid injury to an opponent, and boxers are often shown with severe cuts on their faces (see p. 75).

This type was used for practice during the fourth century BC, but a new glove was evolved for competitions. These gloves were called *sphairai* and consisted of a padded inner bound on by stiff leather thongs. Binding them on must have been a complicated business, and almost immediately after their introduction the first type of ready-made glove, the 'hard' glove, appears. The most distinctive feature of these was a band formed by several thick strips of stout leather encircling the knuckles, making a very effective knuckle-duster. The fingers were left free, but the thonging extended well up the forearm. The colloquial name for these gloves was *myrmykes*, or 'ants', because of their

Two African boxers, one staggering from an upper-cut. 2nd or 1st century BC, height 26.3 cm and 24.4 cm.

Three boxers: two fighting and the other adjusting the thonging of a hard glove. The sheepskin lining is indicated on the forearm. From a Panathenaic amphora, 336 BC.

sting. Often a band of fleece was added round the forearm with which the athlete could wipe off sweat; modern tennis-players use a similar device. These gloves, although formidable, were not nearly as vicious as the Roman *caestus*, which were weighted with iron or lead.

The tactics of ancient boxing were fairly simple. Virtually all blows were directed to the head, while the body was left exposed. The scenes on pottery show that most damage was done to the nose, cheek and chin; pankratiasts or wrestlers were more likely to suffer from a cauliflower ear. Fighting techniques were refined over the years, and a century after the introduction of boxing at Olympia Pythagoras of Samos was said to be the first man to box 'scientifically'. At a later date, when the art of boxing had deteriorated, contestants relied heavily on defensive tactics and were trained to keep their arms up for long periods. Melankomas of Caria, an Olympic victor of the first century AD, is reputed to have been able to keep up his guard for two days, skipping round his opponent without a blow being struck until the other man eventually yielded from exhaustion and sheer frustration. It is no wonder that Melankomas boasted that his face was as unscarred as that of any runner. (Muhammad Ali, the American boxer and Olympic light heavyweight champion in 1960, used the same tactics with great success, inspiring the catch-phrase 'dances like a butterfly, stings like a bee'.)

Various other exercises were performed during training. Shadow-fighting, *skiamachia*, was popular, and the famous boxer Glaukos was honoured with a statue which represented him in this attitude. The medical writer Antyllus recommended that 'the shadow-boxer must not only use his hands but also his legs, sometimes as if he were jumping, at other times as if he were kicking'. Footwork was of course very important: Statius describes how

Alkidamas defeated his heavier opponent Kapaneos by avoiding 'a thousand deaths that flit around his temples by quick movement and by the help of his feet'. Attacking the punch-ball, or *korykos*, was another common exercise; Antyllus proposed that stronger men should have it filled with sand and weaker men with millet or flour. Another effective way to strengthen the muscles was to break up hard ground with a pick, an activity that was necessary to provide a pitch, or *skamma*, for a contest. This type of exertion was so popular among boxers that the pick, or *skapane*, came to be recognized as their symbol (see illustration p. 51).

The most renowned boxer in ancient times was Diagoras of Rhodes, who was of royal descent, and was said to be the tallest man that ever lived. He won once at Olympia (464 BC), twice at Nemea and four times at the Isthmus. He was known as *euthymaches*, the 'fair boxer'. In 448 BC he had the great pleasure of seeing his two sons crowned in the Altis for the *pankration* and boxing. The boys, overjoyed, lifted him on to their shoulders and put both wreaths on his head. One of the crowd shouted, not out of malice but admiration at this ultimate achievement, 'Die now Diagoras; there is nothing left for you but to rise to Olympos.' And there, in his glory, Diagoras collapsed and died.

Several boxers and some wrestlers were regarded as having displayed such super-human strength that they were worshipped as heroes (demi-gods) or even gods. It is no coincidence that Herakles' posthumous deification was consequent upon his completing his twelve great labours of strength: he was the greatest of all strongmen, and Pindar in his Odes often compares athletes to him.

EQUESTRIAN EVENTS

Chariot-races

Then, at the sound of the bronze trumpet, off they started, all shouting to their horses and urging them on with the reins. The clatter of the rattling chariots filled the whole arena, and the dust flew up as they sped along in a dense mass, each driver goading his team unmercifully in his efforts to draw clear of the rival axles and panting steeds, whose steaming breath and sweat drenched every bending back and flying wheel together.

(Sophokles, 5th century BC, *Elektra* 698–760)

This stirring description of a chariot-race shows why this spectacular event remained so popular throughout antiquity. Its modern parallel is Formula 1 racing, equally full of thrills, spills, crashes and fatalities. The glory and prestige attached to victories in the chariot-races were of huge appeal to both states and individuals.

The earliest literary record of a chariot-race is found in the description of the funeral games in Homer's *Iliad*. Chariot-racing, more than any other event, became associated with the passing of the dead into Hades, the Underworld. Only the wealthy aristocrat could afford to equip and maintain a chariot and horses for war or hunting, and to enable him to continue this noble pursuit in the after-life, his chariot and team of horses were often buried or cremated along with him. Excavations have shown that this took place as early as the Mycenaean period.

As noted earlier, athletics festivals probably had their origins in the funeral games held for local heroes. Pelops was the hero of Olympia, and his sanctuary in the Altis was called the Pelopion. Here, during the course of each Olympic festival, rites that included the sacrifice of a black ram were performed in his honour. In mythology Pelops was closely associated with chariot-racing and entered one of the first races to be held at Olympia.

The legendary origin of the equestrian events at Olympia

Oinomaos was King of Pisa, a district not far from Elis, and had a daughter of marriageable age called Hippodameia. Prospective suitors for her hand were required to drive away with her in a chariot. It was agreed that Oinomaos would follow in another chariot, and spear the suitor if he caught up with them. His horses were so swift that the king always succeeded in catching them, and he celebrated his victories by nailing the heads of his unfortunate victims above the palace gateway. The score was twelve when the young Pelops arrived from Phrygia (see p. 10).

There are two alternative versions of what happened next. In the first version Pelops bribed Myrtilos, the royal charioteer, to replace the bronze axle-pins of the king's chariot with wax ones, with the result that Oinomaos was thrown to the ground. He was able to do this because Myrtilos was secretly in love with Hippodameia, but was afraid to challenge her father. Pelops promised him a night with Hippodameia as a reward for his help, but after the victory he showed his gratitude by pitching Myrtilos over a cliff into the sea. It was not necessary for a Greek hero to be virtuous but only to have superhuman strength and cunning. In the second version Poseidon gave Pelops a golden chariot with four winged horses, and in addition caused the wheels to fly off Oinomaos' chariot, so that he was thrown to his death. At the same time the king's palace was struck by lightning and reduced to ashes, save for one wooden pillar that was revered in the Altis for centuries, and stood near what was to be the site of the Temple of Zeus.

Although the pillar was seen by Pausanias it has long since perished, and excavations have not revealed any trace of the palace foundations. It is possible that the pillar was not really part of a building but the finishing post for races that were originally run towards the heart of the sacred grove. This theory is supported by a curious instance of 'accidental archaeology' in Roman times. Pausanias records that a Roman senator, while digging the foundations for the base of his statue near Oinomaos' pillar, came across fragments of arms, bits and bridles. These may have been the offerings of the earliest vic-

Poseidon, lord of the sea, but here the horse's head in his right hand identifies him in another capacity, as patron god of horses. Charioteers and jockeys would offer prayers and sacrifices to him before competing. Roman bronze statuette, height 16.9 cm.

tors in the races, for it was the custom in later years for victors to set up dedications of bronze trappings on the banks of the stadium. A number of these offerings have been found in recent excavations, along with inscriptions recording the name of the donor.

Types of event

The chariot-races were of two types: the *tethrippon* for teams of four horses and the *synoris* for teams of two. Both of these were divided into two separate contests, one for horses of any age, the other for colts. At the *dokimasia*, or inspection, before the Games the judges had to settle any disputes concerning classification into the two groups. On one occasion they disqualified a team entered for the colts' race by a Spartan called Lykinos, because one of the horses was over age, whereupon Lykinos entered his team for the open chariot-race and won. All the races were of gruelling length, ranging from about 4 kilometres for the colts' *synoris* to over 13 kilometres for the open *tethrippon*.

Despite its relatively late introduction to the programme, the *synoris* is likely to have been the oldest type of equestrian event, as it appears on some of the earliest pottery. At Olympia, however, the four-horse chariot-race was the first to be introduced, in 680 BC, while the *synoris* was eventually recognized as an official event in 408 BC, perhaps due to the increasing importance of cavalry fighting at that time.

Thrills and spills

The most hazardous part of the course was undoubtedly the turn. It was crucial to be ahead at the turn, as Nestor advised his son in the Iliad; once this was rounded and you were ahead, you stood a good chance of maintaining the lead. But not everyone was lucky, and Sophokles records what must have been a disastrously familiar occurrence:

ABOVE *Four-horse chariot rounding a post, driven by a charioteer in traditional long white robes. 'Make sure your left-hand horse keeps hard by the turning post', Nestor advised his son before a chariot-race in the Iliad. From a Panathenaic amphora, c.420–400 BC.*

At each turn of the lap, Orestes reined in his inner trace-horse and gave the outer its head, so skilfully that his hub just cleared the post by a hair's breadth every time; and so the poor fellow had safely rounded every lap but one without mishap to himself or his chariot. But at the last he misjudged the turn, slackened his left rein before the horse was safely round the bend, and so struck the post. The hub was smashed across, and he was hurled over the rail entangled in the reins, and as he fell his horses ran wild across the course.

(Sophokles, 5th century BC, *Elektra* 698–760)

LEFT *The wreckage of a four-horse chariot, with two of the horses completely overthrown and the driver pitched from his chariot, which is shown above in the background, in profile. Etruscan carnelian scaraboid sealstone, 5th century BC, length 1.3cm.*

Just before the chariots reached the turning post, they had to pass the taraxippos, or 'horse-terrorizer'. This was a circular altar at the edge of the south bank which Pausanias says struck panic into the horses and caused many a disaster. He records many local legends to explain the phenomenon, but since other hippodromes had similar features (though none as terrifying as that at Olympia, says Pausanias), a more rational explanation seems necessary. One modern suggestion is that, since the equestrian events began at sunrise, both horses and drivers would have had the sun directly in their eyes as the chariots sped along the southern track. When they reached the altar, which was situated just before the turn, the tension and bewilderment would have been at a climax. The position of the altar itself was therefore either purely coincidental or deliberately placed at the site of many a disaster.

Bronze model of a two-horse chariot, of which only one horse remains. Roman, height 18.6 cm.

The chariots

The chariots themselves appear to have been of such slender construction, without springing, that it is easy to imagine how continual bumping over rutted ground would jar every bone in the driver's body. The four-horse racing-chariot was an adaptation of the Homeric two-horse war-chariot, but lighter, to increase speed, and smaller, as it carried only one person. The middle pair of horses *(zygioi)* were harnessed to a yoke, which was fastened to the pole, and secured by a strap to the rim of the chariot. The outer pair of horses were trace-horses *(seiraphoroi)*. The charioteer carried a whip or a goad, sometimes together with a long stick with metal jingles on the end, and the horses were controlled by reins and bits, or alternatively nose-bands. The two-horse chariot was generally similar to the four-horse, although the Athenians used a variation, consisting merely of a seat for the driver with an open framework at the back and sides, and a footboard suspended from the pole. This was similar to the chariot that was used for the mule-cart race (see illustration p. 87). The chariots were usually made of wood, wickerwork (probably brightly painted) and leather thonging, and were sometimes decorated with sheet-bronze cladding and finials, occasionally inlaid with silver.

Miniature bronze chariot-wheels. Modest offerings like these are likely to have been made by charioteers rather than by owners of teams. One is dedicated to Zeus by a certain Eudamas and probably commemorates a victory in the Games at Nemea where it was found. 5th century BC, diameter (both) 10.1 cm.

The charioteers

At the athletic festivals the charioteers were rarely the owners of their chariot and teams. They were usually employed in much the same way as racehorse owners now employ jockeys. Chariot-driving was an extremely hazardous affair, and unless you were a particular devotee of the sport it was not worth risking your own life. In the case of victory, the owner still received all the glory, including the crown and the twin honours of being announced by the herald as the winner and of being recorded in the list of victors, while the driver had to be content with the victory ribbon. In exceptional circumstances the charioteer might be celebrated along with the owner in an ode specially commissioned for the occasion, or he might even be represented in the victory monument. It was considered very honourable to drive your own team, and in one of his Odes Pindar congratulates Herodotos of Thebes for doing this. In the fifth century BC Damonon of Sparta boasted in an inscription that he and his son Enymakratidas had won a total of sixty-eight victories in chariot- and horse-races at eight different festivals.

The mule-cart race

The Eleans apparently did not approve of the introduction of this race, known as the *apene*, and it lasted for only fourteen Olympiads. The influential Greeks from Sicily were probably responsible for this innovation at Olympia, as that country was famous for its mules. The event is often depicted on Sicilian coins and one Sicilian victor is perhaps celebrated in one of Pindar's Odes. In Elis, however, there was an ancient curse on mules bred within the territory; in view of the religious conservatism of the Games the Eleans possibly frowned upon such a race but it continued as an Olympic event for the next fifty-six years.

ABOVE *Silver coin struck for a victory in the mule-cart race at Olympia in either 484 or 480 BC by Anaxilas of Rhegium (494–476 BC). The high, box-like seat was peculiar to mule-carts.*

The horse-races

The mare of Pheidolas the Corinthian was called...Aura and, although her rider was thrown at the beginning of the race, she ran straight on and turned at the pillar; when she heard the sound of the trumpet, she ran on all the faster and beat the other horses. The Eleans proclaimed Pheidolas the victor, and allowed him to dedicate this statue of the mare.

(Pausanias, 2nd century AD, *Description of Greece* VI 13.9)

From this story one might imagine that the horse which won at Olympia received as much adulation as our Derby winner. Horse-racing in antiquity was just as exciting and even more dangerous than it is today. The jockeys rode bare-back and without stirrups – these and the saddle had not yet been invented; moreover, at the Olympic festival the horse-races took place after the chariot events, so that the ground was already well churned and rutted.

LEFT *Harnessing-up. The collar for the trace-horse hangs down on this side. Water-jar, c.520–500 BC.*

A jubilant young victor after a horse-race. A groom holds up the crown for all to see and bears away on his head the prize, a high-handled tripod. A herald walks before the horse proclaiming the victor: 'The horse of Dusnikeitos wins.' Greek amphora, c.520–500 BC.

One ancient writer claimed that for many people the greatest thrills in horse-racing were provided by the mishaps that befell the competitors, and it is unlikely that they were often disappointed. Galen was only too familiar with the consequences of hard riding which included injuries to the chest, the kidneys and reproductive organs, 'to say nothing of the stumbling of the horses, which has often pitched riders from their seat, instantly killing them'.

It should be no surprise to learn that jockeys, like charioteers, were usually

Life-size statue of a bronze horse at full gallop with diminutive jockey (compare the boys on race-horses on the frontispiece vase). Found off Cape Artemision, south of the island of Euboea, 3rd–2nd century BC.

BELOW *Bronze statuette of a rider dismounting during the* anabates *race, one of four similar statuettes from the rim of a bronze cinerary urn. Various types of horse-racing were popular in both Greece and Italy. Etrusco-Campanian, 500–480 BC.*

paid servants. Some owners did compete themselves: horse-sports, after all, were an ancient and aristocratic pastime. Military leaders in particular tended to be expert horsemen. Themistokles taught his sons to ride, throw javelins standing on horseback, and perform other dangerous feats. Aristophanes was critical of 'horsey' young men (see p. 97), and a passionate interest in racing is confirmed by the price paid for a race-horse in 421 BC: 1,200 drachmai, at least three times the average annual wage. For the wealthy young man in antiquity a fast horse was just as essential as today's fast car.

Types of race

The ordinary horse-race was run over six stades, a little under 1,200 metres. There were also two other equestrian events at Olympia. These were a race for colts and another for mares, called the *calpe* or *anabates* ('dismounter'). In the latter the rider dismounted for the last stretch and ran beside his horse. Its origins were probably military, since speed and agility were essential for a horseman in battle. It is interesting that a similar event is included in our gymkhanas.

7 PRIZE-GIVING AND CELEBRATIONS

PRIZES AND CEREMONIES

Marble statue of a young athlete binding on a victor's ribbons. Roman copy of a Greek bronze original of about 440 BC, height 1.38 metres.

T he greatest achievement for an athlete in the ancient world was to win the Olympic crown. The material prizes offered at other athletic festivals were insignificant compared to the fame and glory earned by the Olympic victor.

The sacred olive tree (plan p. 14, 5) from which the wreaths were made stood amid a cluster to the rear of the Temple of Zeus. King Iphitos of Elis had offered a wreath as a prize on the instruction of the Delphic Oracle, which told him to go to Olympia and search for the tree decked in gossamer webs (cobwebs were considered to be a sign of rain and they were therefore connected with fertility). Iphitos returned to Olympia, found the tree and encircled it with a fence. It came to be known as the *kotinos kallistephanos*, 'the olive beautiful for its crowns'. According to Aristotle, it was remarkable because its leaves grew in a symmetrical pattern like the myrtle and because, unlike other olives, the leaves were pale green on the upper side and not, as is usual, on the underside. Before each festival it was the custom for a young boy whose parents were still alive to cut the branches with a golden sickle. One branch was cut for each contest so that the victor's crown could be made from it.

It is uncertain where and when the crowning took place. There is evidence for two different ceremonies held at different stages in the history of the Games.

According to one account the victors were crowned immediately after the competition. This must have been the practice in later times, for when in AD 107 the boxer Apollonius arrived late for his contest, he found that he had been disqualified and the crown was already

A winner is presented with tokens of victory: palm branches and fillets, or woollen ribbons, which were tied round the head, arms or legs. From a Greek drinking-cup, about 500–475 BC.

BELOW *A winged figure representing Victory crowns an athlete with an olive wreath; in his hand is an olive branch. Cast from a sealstone, 2nd or 1st century BC, 23 x 16 mm.*

in place on the head of his opponent Herakleides. Enraged, he bound on his boxing thongs and started a vicious attack on him.

Pausanias records that in the Temple of Hera there was a gold and ivory table designed by Kolotes, a pupil of Pheidias, on which the wreaths for the victors were displayed. The table may have been taken to the stadium for the prize-giving ceremony; there would have been ample space for it in front of the seats on the judges' stand (see drawing p. 31).

According to another version, which has been adopted for the programme given on p. 53, the victors were not crowned until a special ceremony at the end of the festival held in front of the statue in the Temple of Zeus. In the meantime ribbons of wool were tied around the athlete's head, arms and legs as a mark of victory, and at a later date he was also given a palm branch.

FEASTING

And the whole company raised a great cheer, while the lovely light of the fair-faced moon lit up the evening. Then, in joyful celebration, the whole Altis rang with banquet-song.

(Pindar, 5th century BC, *Olympian Odes* X 73–8)

In addition to the public banquet for victors, there were various private celebrations in the evenings. The wine flowed, and there were songs and revelry. Victors and friends alike decked themselves in garlands and processed

BELOW *A drinking party: revellers play a game of* kottabos, *which entailed flinging the dregs in their wine-cups* (kylikes) *at a target. Others drink wine from deep cups* (skyphoi). *In the background hang baskets for cheese, a* kylix *and a cheetah-skin case for musical double-pipes.*

BOTTOM *Five youths dance to the music of the double pipes and fill their drinking-cups with wine from a mixing-bowl, or* krater. *From a Greek drinking-cup, c.500–475 BC, height 10.1 cm.*

Inscription on a stone slab commemorating the achievements of a Roman athlete named Lucius who 'won at the Didymaean Games, competed for the crown at Olympia and competed in all the other athletic festivals in a manner worthy of victory'. Height 80 cm.

round the Altis singing victory hymns, which were either time-honoured chants or odes specially composed for the occasion by leading poets such as Pindar or Bacchylides. The wealthier the victor the larger and more luxurious the celebration. Both Alkibiades of Athens and Anaxilas of Rhegion provided magnificent feasts to celebrate their victories. Empedokles of Agrigentum was a disciple of Pythagoras and accordingly a vegetarian. He made an ox of dough garnished with costly herbs and spices, and distributed it among the spectators. Often the party continued all night, and on the following morning the victors (who one hopes were not competing again that day) made solemn vows and sacrifices to the appropriate gods.

HOMEWARD-BOUND

After the feasting on the final day there remained the problem of getting home. One is reminded of present-day chaos after a football match when Lucian complains that he could not get a wagon 'because too many people were departing at the same time'.

Although the Games had come to an end, the fame of the victor lived on. His statue was erected in the Altis, provided of course that he could afford it himself, or it was paid for by his friends, relations or the state. Hundreds of these statues were dedicated but now after the ravages of time very little remains except bases and small fragments. Were it not for Pausanias, we would know very little about this vast open-air art gallery.

An athlete might also be commemorated by a statue set up in his home-town. In addition he would often be allowed to dine for life at public expense; he would be given sums of money and granted civic honours. On his return from the Games he was given a civic reception followed by further feasting and celebrations. Exainetos of Akragas in Sicily, who won the stade-race for a second time in 420 BC, was escorted in procession by 300 chariots drawn by white horses.

The most celebrated athletes had grand burials, as we now know from that of an athlete at Taranto, who was buried wearing a gold wreath in a sarcophagus surrounded by four Panathenaic amphorae. A pathological examination has indicated that he may have been a discus-thrower, even perhaps identifiable with Ikkos (see pp. 46, 47).

8 POLITICS, SCANDAL AND PROPAGANDA

It is a wonder that anyone has so little respect for the god of Olympia as to offer or take bribes in the contests: it is even more of a wonder that one of the Eleans themselves has fallen so low.

(Pausanias, 2nd century AD, v 21, 16–17)

The approach of each modern Olympics inevitably provokes a comparison between the perceived simplicity and idealism of the original Olympics and the lavish, high-security spectacle of the modern Games. Place the ancient Games under close scrutiny, however, and we can discern elements of bribery, corruption, scandal, political intrusion, propaganda and profiteering – precisely the problems that beleaguer the modern Games.

Even before the influence of the Romans, with their love of grandiose public entertainment, the ancient Greek contests were a big news event, drawing tens of thousands of spectators and turning top athletes into living legends. The enthusiasm of the classical world for sport was such that not only was there one major Greek national Games event every year (p. 11) but other Greek localities sponsored smaller meets, and by Roman times hundreds of sports festivals around the Mediterranean had been granted 'Olympic' status, their events and programmes modelled closely on the original.

FAME AND WEALTH FOR THE WINNERS

The Greeks traditionally believed that athletes received their prowess in part from the gods and therefore it was to the gods that athletes prayed for victory and offered gifts, both to curry favour and in gratitude. From as early as the fourth century BC, however, the inscriptions on the stone bases of the victors' statues begin to tell us a different story: it was already the athletes themselves and their city-states who were receiving primary recognition.

At the major games the only prizes were symbolic honours: crowns of olive at Olympia, laurel at Delphi, fresh celery and later pine at Corinth, and dried celery at Nemea. The victors' home states, however, provided ample cash rewards, along with such civic honours as free board and lodging and theatre seats, not to mention, by the third and second centuries BC, extravagant receptions and parades. The Athenian legislator Solon had decreed that Athenian winners at the Isthmian and Olympic Games should receive cash rewards - 100 drachmai for Isthmian and 500 drachmai for Olympic victories (an income of 500 drachmai per annum would have placed an Athenian in the top earning bracket). Sometimes states would erect statues of their victors at the location where they won their victories or in their hometowns. This was no mean reward, for a life-size statue in bronze or marble could cost the equivalent of ten years' wages for the average worker. Doubtless some of the wealthier victors financed their own monuments: one man, Dikon, had fifteen statues, equal to his number of Olympic wins.

States would sometimes pay for an athlete's training, and there are even instances of top athletes being 'bought' by city-states that hoped to benefit from athletic or equestrian triumphs. The wealthy Greek colonies of southern Italy and Sicily had a very strong penchant for sports, in which they invested heavily, particularly in the equestrian events and by recruiting athletes from other cities. In the early fifth century BC Astylos of Croton (in southern Italy), victor in the long-distance race and in the race-in-armour, mysteriously changed his national allegiance to Syracuse (in Sicily) between one Olympics and the next, while in the fourth century BC a Syracusan tyrant tried to bribe the father of a winner in the boys' boxing contest to have the boy proclaimed a Syracusan. Similarly, the city of Ephesus in Asia Minor succeeded in acquiring a Cretan long-distance runner after his second Olympic victory.

While the expense of maintaining horses and equipping a team meant that only the wealthy could compete in chariot races, a young athlete from the lower classes could probably work his way up to the top in other athletics events. The first known Olympic victor, Koroibos, is recorded as a cook, while other early victors included a cowherd and a goatherd. There were no regulations prohibiting professional athletes from competing at the ancient games, and a successful athlete probably could have earned his living simply by travelling around from one athletics event to another. While cash prizes were not given at the Olympics themselves, elsewhere a single sprint race could earn the winner a prize large enough to buy a luxury house. Celebrity sportsmen were occasionally paid huge fees by entrepreneurs to appear at local festivals, in one case as much as five talents, the equivalent of about 27 kg of silver. At the Great Panathenaic festival in Athens, held every four years in honour of Athena, patron goddess of the city, vast quantities of olive oil were presented as prizes. The olive oil was contained in amphorae decorated with illustrations of the goddess Athena on one side and the contest at which the prize was won on the other. The oil was used for lighting, heating and cooking, and for cleansing and lubricating the body. The vessels, with or without oil, were occasionally sold, often to buyers in Italy. Athletes were apparently allowed to export vessels without paying the usual duty. Each vessel was worth a minimum of twelve days' wages, and the biggest prize, for the sprint, was one hundred amphorae with an estimated value of many thousands of pounds.

Famous poets, notably Pindar the great Greek lyricist, were paid large sums to write songs in the victors' honour. Wins were recorded with pride on athletes' epitaphs and in stone inscriptions that hailed them as benefactors of the state. As already discussed (p. 62), the names of the winners in the Olympic foot-race were even used as a dating system for the four-year periods, or Olympiads, by tradition going back to 776 BC. In this respect it is essential to remember that the prime objective at the ancient Olympics was to come first: second or third places counted for nothing and were not even recorded.

POLITICS AND SPORT

Etruscan bronze helmet found at Olympia in 1817, inscribed 'Hieron, son of Deinomenes and the Syracusans [dedicated] to Zeus Etruscan [spoils] from Cumae'. Hieron I of Syracuse had assisted the Greeks to win a massive naval battle against the Etruscans off the coast of Cumae in 474 BC. In a poem written in honour of Hieron's success in a chariot-race at Delphi in 470 BC, Pindar described the naval victory as freeing the Greeks from slavery. About 500–480 BC, height 21 cm.

The national sanctuaries were cultural and religious centres that provided arenas not only for sporting events but also for music, dance, drama and public debate. Olympia was crammed with temples and altars to the gods, as well as treasury buildings where city-states and colonies could display their wealth; and to impress visitors, states erected monuments to their deities, athletes, statesmen, heroes and military triumphs. Although the Eleans, in whose territory the sanctuary of Olympia was situated, were of minor political significance, they inevitably became embroiled in hostilities as a result of their role in the festival, and the problems of this are documented from at least as early as the fifth century BC (p. 99).

The ancient gymnasia and sports festivals were ideal as political forums, and often statesmen used the occasion of the Olympic festival to deliver an oration to the assembled masses. The admiral Themistokles enjoyed a spectacular welcome at the first Olympic festival after the Persian Wars, which had culminated in his victory at the Battle of Salamis in 480 BC. He so captured the admiration of the assembled crowds that for the rest of that day it was he who had their attention rather than the Games. The historian Herodotos also read his account of the Persian Wars here. In 324 BC, Alexander the Great chose Olympia for the announcement of his edict for the safe return of all Greek exiles to their native cities. Here, too, in 388 BC Lysias delivered his 'Olympic Oration', through which he succeeded in persuading the Greeks to rout his fellow-countryman, the tyrant Dionysios of Syracuse, who had wreaked havoc and destruction after seizing control of the whole of south-western Italy. Dionysios had sent several teams of horses to be entered at the Games, professional speakers to recite his poems, and a tent decorated with golden thread and furnished with vivid carpets to house his delegates. As an immediate response to Lysias' incitement, the crowd opened hostilities by creating uproar during the recitals and by looting the magnificent tent.

Athletes themselves occasionally served as political envoys or, like the modern British runner Sebastian Coe, took up politics after their retirement. Such was the case of Theagenes of Thasos, a boxer and wrestler who ventured into public affairs after a stunning sports career spanning more than twenty years, with twenty-three victories in the circuit games and more than a thousand at lesser festivals. Unfortunately, his successes, if not the rigours of his sport, seem to have gone to his head, for he also began to proclaim himself the son of the demi-god Herakles.

A powerfully built stallion wearing a lioness or panther skin pulls back from a black groom trying to control him with a whip. This impressive relief (possibly a tomb monument), showing a prized horse, was found at Plateia Kolonos in Athens. Marble relief, 3rd–2nd century BC, height 1.99 metres.

OPPORTUNITIES FOR SPONSORSHIP AND SELF-ADVERTISEMENT

Equestrian events were the showiest and most magnificent and provided ample opportunities for propaganda. Sometimes chariot entries were financed not by individuals but by states: in 472 BC, for example, the 'public chariot' of the Argives won an Olympic victory. The investment was good publicity for a state that specialized in horse-breeding. The extensive plains of Argos, Euboea and Thessaly and the area around Athens were renowned for their breeds of horses, but most famous of all were those of Sicily and southern Italy. In those parts horse sports were the passionate love of the local princes. They tried to gain popularity and influence with the crowds at major festivals by entering teams of horses in the Games and making numerous dedications. The well-known bronze charioteer of Delphi was part of a chariot-group dedicated by a Syracusan tyrant, probably soon after 474 BC.

To ensure victory it was not unusual for an individual to enter a number of chariots in one race. In 416 BC the Athenian politician Alkibiades entered seven chariots at the Olympic Games, taking first, second and either third or fourth place. Aristophanes could easily have had him in mind when he ridiculed the fashionable young Athenians who spent vast sums on horses, affected horsey names (all those beginning 'Hipp-') and spoke of virtually nothing but horses all day. Alkibiades' enemies levelled all kinds of charges against him, including one of taking a fellow-competitor's horses. At the time Alkibiades was seeking generalship in a proposed invasion of Sicily, and retaliated strongly, claiming that, whereas the Greeks had thought Athens to be weakened by the Peloponnesian War, they now exaggerated her power because of his exceptional performance at the Olympic Games. Political propaganda is by no means peculiar to the modern Olympics.

Alkibiades was not the only Athenian general addicted to chariot-racing. Cimon, the father of the great Miltiades, won the four-horse chariot-race at three successive Olympic Games, in 532, 528 and 524 BC. His horses were honoured not only with bronze statues but with burial in the family tomb.

WERE THE JUDGES BEYOND SUSPICION?

As for bribery, there is indisputable evidence from antiquity of corruption among a minority of competitors and of the severe punishment with which such instances were met (p. 39), but there is only one known occasion where the judges themselves were compromised. Contrary to the present situation, the Olympics had a permanent home, and so there were no inducements offered to the judges and officials by would-be hosts. Such was the concern for impartiality in the Olympic administration that, as Herodotos relates, in the early sixth century BC a delegation from Elis visited the Pharaoh Psammis in Egypt seeking advice on how to improve the organization of the Games. After consultation with his advisers Psammis proffered that true impartiality could only be achieved if the Eleans themselves were excluded from the Games. It is uncertain whether this proposal was ever adopted, and it is a little surprising that until the fourth century BC the judges were allowed to enter horses in the equestrian events. In 372 BC, however, when the Elean

Bronze plaque from a statue of Troilos, who was both a judge and an Olympic winner. The inscription, in verse, reads: 'I was Hellanodikes at Olympia when Zeus granted my first Olympic victory with prize-winning horses and then my second in succession, again with horses. Troilos was the son of Alkinoos.' Pausanias records that the statue at Olympia was made by the great sculptor Lysippos and that Troilos won two chariot-races in 372 BC. Troilos, as owner of the horses, was thus proclaimed victor in the same contests over which he presided.
Height 8 cm.

Troilos won victories in both the two-horse chariot-race and the four-horse colts' race, the Eleans finally decided to ban judges' horses from the competitions.

The awe and respect in which the Elean authorities were generally held seems to have precluded any unwarranted interference, with one notorious exception. The Emperor Nero had the Games postponed from AD 65 to AD 67, and appeared with a ten-horse team, only to be thrown from his chariot. He was helped to remount but still failed to finish, yet even so he was proclaimed victor, on the grounds that he would have won had he been able to complete the course. Matters were, however, rectified: after his death in AD 68 the Games were declared invalid and Nero's name was expunged from the victor-lists. His successor Galba also insisted that a 250,000-drachma bribe to the judges, to whom Nero had also awarded Roman citizenship, should be paid back.

9 DEATH AND REBIRTH

THE END OF THE ANCIENT OLYMPIC GAMES

The Games were introduced as a religious ceremony in honour of Zeus, but as time went by, belief in the traditional religion faded, and the Games lost their religious significance. The ideology behind the Games reached its zenith in the fifth century BC. During this period the neutrality of the Eleans ensured their control of the festival. In the course of the Peloponnesian War the Eleans abandoned their neutrality and sided with the Athenians, banning the Spartans from the Games. Subsequently, in 424 BC under threat of invasion by the Spartans, the Games were held under the protection of thousands of armed troops. The invasion did not in fact take place, but the precautions that had been considered necessary indicated that the authority of the Sacred Truce was on the wane. The religious and nationalistic unity of the Greeks was disintegrating.

In 365 BC the Arcadians, aided by the Pisatans, the old enemies of Elis, seized control of Olympia and occupied the sanctuary. In the following year, when the Arcadians and the Pisatans staged the Games, the Eleans tried unsuccessfully to regain the sanctuary by force. During the siege the forces occupying the Altis plundered the temples in order to pay their mercenaries. Power was restored to the Eleans only when it was feared that the wrath of the gods would be incurred. The coin shown on p. 10 came from the first issue to be struck by the Eleans after the Pisatan 'interlude'.

Although the sanctity of the Olympic Games was preserved for a little longer, men were beginning to usurp the sovereignty of the gods; the athletes credited themselves and not Zeus with their victories. When the Philippeion was constructed in 336 BC, it was adorned with gold and ivory statues of Alexander the Great and his family; previously these materials had been reserved for statues of the gods. In later years the Romans converted the Temple of Rhea into a shrine in honour of Rome and the 'divine Augustus'. Two centuries separated these two events, during which time Rome had incorporated the Greek mainland into her empire, and internal strife between Roman political parties took its toll of Greek culture. The Altis suffered most damage at the hands of the Roman general Sulla, who sacked not only Olympia but also Delphi and Epidauros to finance his wars against the Persian king Mithridates. In order to celebrate the successful conclusion of the war he transferred the Olympic Games to Rome in 80 BC. Following his death two years later, however, the festival was returned to its proper site. For a time the Games took on a new lease of life; Roman interest in sport,

Interior of Pheidias' workshop, converted into a church in the Byzantine period. This was where Pheidias may have prepared the great gold and ivory statue of Zeus (see p. 20).

and money invested in ostentatious monuments in the sanctuary, helped Olympia to regain its old prestige, but this did not prevent Caligula from trying to have Zeus's gold and ivory statue removed to Rome.

Henceforth it was almost as if the gods had deserted Olympia, and its fortunes declined. In AD 267 the Heruli, a tribe from southern Russia, invaded the Peloponnese, and the Eleans tried to save the most sacred part of the Altis. They hastily built a wall to enclose the area between the temple of Zeus and the Bouleuterion, robbing stone from the buildings on the edge of the sanctuary to complete it. The sanctuary was never restored to its previous grandeur. It is not certain when the last festival was celebrated. A bronze plaque recently found in the gymnasium names victors as late as the 380s, including an Armenian prince. It was perhaps no later than AD 393, when Theodosius I, the first Christian Emperor of Rome, banned all pagan cults, or they may have continued until the Temple of Zeus was burnt down in approximately AD 426, possibly in accordance with the edict of Theodosius II who ordered all pagan temples in the eastern Mediterranean to be destroyed. Between the fifth and eighth centuries AD successive waves of invaders – Visigoths, Avars, Vandals and Slavs – laid waste to the Altis, which in time was totally devastated by earthquakes, floods and landslides. It was to be another thousand years before archaeologists excavated the fertile ground of Olympia and replanted in men's minds the seeds of the Olympic ideal.

REVIVALS OF THE GAMES

Despite the likely abolition of the Games at Olympia by the 390s AD, the events lived on. In the Byzantine period a re-creation of the Games took place in Constantinople (Istanbul), capital of the eastern half of the Roman Empire. Presumably, now separated from their pagan origins, the Games were deemed acceptable. Ironically, though, the great cult statue of Zeus, which was looted early in the fifth century AD, was reconstructed in the palace of the Chamberlain Lausus in Istanbul, where it remained with other cult statues taken from Greek sanctuaries until the palace was destroyed by fire in AD 475. Here the Games were held in the Hippodrome, the heart of Roman social and political life. The Roman love of chariot-racing made it dominant in the much altered programme: it was the most popular event and seems to have been held on the slightest pretext — on regular dates as well as on military triumphs and even military reverses, on religious festivals, on Sundays and on the emperor's birthday, sometimes lasting the morning, sometimes all day. Mock battles, hunts and acrobatics were also staged, but despite the overwhelming preoccupation with show and spectacle, the basic athletic contests continued to be held: wrestling, boxing, discus, long-jump and the foot-race (still considered an important event), along with four open events, javelin, weight-lifting, archery and shot-put.

The start of the modern Olympics

The first modern Olympic Games were held in Athens in 1896 at the instigation of a French nobleman, Baron Pierre de Coubertin. From an early age he had taken a keen interest in educational systems and was a firm believer in the parallel development of mind and body. During the course of the nineteenth century many countries had begun to recognize the importance of physical exercise, but it had little following in France. Coubertin had long been distressed by the low morale of his countrymen after the defeat of Louis Napoleon at Sedan in 1870 during the Franco-Prussian War. In the 1880s Coubertin launched into a series of articles and speeches extolling the virtues of British education and emphasizing its concentration on the sporting disciplines. He had visited England and was impressed by the high standard of physical and intellectual education; he also read the works of Dr Thomas Arnold, headmaster of Rugby from 1828 to 1842, and strongly approved of the curriculum at the school, where competitive games and sport were compulsory. More influential still on Coubertin were the 'Olympic Games' held at Much Wenlock in Shropshire. The Much Wenlock Olympian Society, founded in 1850 by Dr William Penny Brookes (1809–95), became the Shropshire Olympian Society in 1861. Coubertin visited Much Wenlock in 1890, planted an oak tree and later wrote that the revival of the Olympic Games was due more to Brookes than to any other person. Coubertin was also influenced by the gymnastic traditions of Scandinavia and Germany. But his faith in the virtues of Anglo-Saxon education was reinforced by his visit to the Ivy League universities of the United States in 1890, where he was impressed by the scale and excellence of American collegiate sport.

Pierre de Fredi, Baron de Coubertin (1863–1937), who initiated the revival of the Olympic Games in 1896.

The marble stadium at Athens, reconstructed for the staging of the first modern Olympic Games in 1896. The stadium is now no longer used for official track races, its bends at each end being too tight, but it still serves as the finish of the annual Marathon–Athens marathon.

Coubertin's imagination was further fired by reports of the early excavations at Olympia, and finally, at an assembly of French sportsmen at the Sorbonne in 1892, he proposed the re-establishment of the Games in a move to revive national prestige by rekindling the competitive spirit of the ancient Olympics. At first the idea met with little enthusiasm. But Coubertin persisted and in 1894 he organized a splendid banquet for an international meeting of sportsmen and physical education enthusiasts from seventy-nine countries. Lit by a thousand torches and marked by horse-races, mock battles and fireworks, the extravaganza aroused the participants to rapturous acclaim of Coubertin's proposal. This meeting of the International Athletic Conference, which was to become the IOC, the International Olympic Committee, opened with the Hymn to Apollo, allegedly based on ancient music notation recently discovered by French archaeologists at Delphi, and this caused a huge impact on the assembled audience.

With the approval of King George I of Greece, Athens was chosen as the host city for the first new Games; famed in antiquity, it had grown up as a new city and as capital of Greece over the previous fifty years. A neglected hollow on the city outskirts, all that remained of a marble stadium donated in the second century AD by wealthy Roman Herodes Atticus, became the site of a new marble stadium financed by an Alexandrian merchant.

The spectacles and musical productions that accompanied the 1896 Games far outshone the athletic performances. The facilities were poor, and only the English and the Americans recognized the need for substantial training and preparation, though fittingly the hero of the Athens Olympics was a Greek farmer, Spyridione Loues, who was victorious in the marathon. He was greeted by a hundred thousand cheering onlookers, most of them his fellow-countrymen. After a break of some 1,500 years the overwhelming adulation which greeted this humble athlete provides a glimpse of how the winner must have been fêted all those centuries ago: a barber declared that he would provide him with a shave for the rest of his life; he was promised hats from a hatter, shoes from a shoe-maker, underwear and socks from a haberdasher, free meals, free drinks and theatre tickets, and all these favours until his dying day; even a smallholding was given to him by a rich landowner.

Relatively few countries participated in the 1896 Games, and relatively few of the spectators came from abroad. The Greek royal family, however, saw the opportunity to increase their own prestige by the birth of this international event, and it was with some difficulty that Coubertin wrested the modern Games from a permanent setting in Greece, motivated largely by a desire for the 1900 Olympics to be held at the great Universal Exposition in Paris.

Coubertin's vision had involved not only the promotion of sport but a marriage of athletics and art, again inspired by the artists', architects' and musicians' competitions which had taken place in antiquity. Although efforts were made at some of the early modern Olympics to arrange cultural events to coincide with the Games, by 1920 Coubertin himself acknowledged that these had not been a success; it became evident that neither writers nor musicians were interested, and sculptors produced work which he found to be 'comic, rather than anything else'. Nonetheless, the modern Olympics have inspired a great many medals, posters and stamps of exceptional standard, and masterpieces perhaps undreamed of by Coubertin, including in

The 'Biel Throne'. Marble judge's seat from the Panathenaic stadium in Athens, as rebuilt by Herodes Atticus, AD 140–53. On the side is an olive-tree and a prize-table with a Panathenaic amphora and three wreaths. Two owls form the legs. Given in 1801 by the Archbishop of Athens to Mr and Mrs Hamilton Nisbet, whose family kept it at Biel, Lothian. Purchased by the British Museum with a grant from the Olympic Museum, Lausanne. Height 70 cm.

Silver medal presented by the Swedish Olympic Committee, commemorating the Olympic Games in Stockholm in 1912. The seated statue of Zeus is shown against a background of the city of Stockholm. Designed by Erik Lindberg.

the field of cinematography the film of the 1936 Berlin Olympics, *Olympische Spiele* by Leni Riefenstahl.

Earlier Greek Olympics

The 1896 Olympics, however, did not constitute the first attempt to re-stage the event. As far back as the 1830s the idea was mooted in Greece, following the liberation of Greece from the Turks and the founding of the modern Greek state. In 1837 a royal decree gave legal status to athletic events as part of industrial exhibitions, but it was not until the 1850s that funding promised by Evangelos Zappas came to fruition, and the first festival was held in 1859, including running races, discus, javelin, wrestling and climbing. The games were subsequently held in 1870, 1875 and 1888, with the winners receiving cash, medals and olive-branches.

The Cotswold 'Olimpick Games'

In the early years of the seventeenth century (the exact date is unknown) the English barrister Robert Dover, with the permission of King James I, organized the first Cotswold 'Olimpick Games' on a hill near Chipping Campden. Like the original Olympics, they were probably a formalization of local sports that had already been in existence for some time. There was a growing trend in England at the time to empathise with the ancient Greeks whom they much admired, but the real reason for Dover's establishment of the games, again echoing the purpose of ancient sports, may have been military. He wished to persuade the Puritans, who formed the parliamentary opposition to the king and associated sports with immorality, drunkenness and festivals of pagan origins, that physical exercise was essential for the defence of the realm.

The main events of the Cotswold Olimpicks, despite their Hellenic leanings, had a truly English flavour: of primary importance were horse-racing, hunting and coursing with hounds, but there were also athletic events including running, jumping, javelin-throwing, sledge-hammer throwing, wrestling, fencing with sticks or cudgels, and shin-kicking. Women took part in the gentler events such as dancing, but later they also had their own running race, 'the smock race', for which the prize was a be-ribboned holland tunic; they performed the actual race, however, 'in a dress hardly reconcileable to the rules of decency' (Richard Graves, *The Spiritual Quixote*, 1773).

Frontispiece of the Annalia Dubrensia (1636), illustrating the events of the Cotswold Olimpicks. Taking its title from the Latin form of Robert Dover's surname, this was a collection of poems by Michael Drayton, Ben Jonson and others, which provided an early record of the games. Dover is shown as Master of Ceremonies, mounted on a white horse and bearing his wand of office.

Wrestling at the Cotswold Olimpicks in the early 18th century. The musician seated in the tree is Twangdillo, a one-legged, one-eyed fiddler who provided music for the events (a practice reminiscent of pipe-players accompanying ancient sports). The dress or holland tunic hanging from a ridge-pole above the wrestlers was the prize for the women's running race.

The bulk of the contests were open to all and sundry, from the nobility to labourers, and winners were adorned with yellow ribbons – such was their cachet that some of them were worn all year. The competitions were accompanied by dancing, song and great festivity. The atmosphere and celebration of these games, with their ale-booths, stalls, musicians, acrobats, itinerant quack doctors, pedlars and mix of serious and semi-comic events may have been more akin to the original Olympics than any parallel which we have now (cf. p. 52). A musician dressed as Homer played a harp and sang, an allusion to the Olympic connection with which Dover had sought to ennoble his games, and in the *Annalia Dubrensia*, an anthology dedicated to Dover and his games published in 1636, there is reference to the renown of the Greeks and the ancient Olympics. The finale was a grand firework display centred on a temporary castle-like structure, on which were mounted guns used to start the contests.

The Cotswold Olimpicks were held annually but came to a halt temporarily with the Civil War in 1644 and with Dover's death in 1652. They recommenced in 1660, to be held annually until 1852, with varying quality and eventually with an increase in popularity and boisterousness which might have vindicated Puritan disapproval. Fresh interest in the Olimpicks in more recent times eventually led to the setting-up of the Robert Dover's Games Society in 1965, and the games have been re-established on a local basis with much success and with a determination to retain the distinctive character of the games, resisting expansion and commercialism.

Yet more attempts

Other more ephemeral versions of the Olympic Games have also been introduced at various times and places: apart from the Much Wenlock games mentioned above (p. 101), another was staged at Hampton Court in 1679, and 'Olympic Festival Events' were held in Liverpool between 1852 and 1867. England was not the only country to revive the ancient games; the late eighteenth and nineteenth centuries saw re-births of the Olympics at various locations in Europe and America: at the Champs de Mars in Paris (1770), in Wörlitz-Dessau in Germany (1779), in the Grand Duchy of Posnan in Poland

(1830), at Ramlösa in Sweden (1834, 1836), in Montreal (1844), in New York at the Franconi Hippodrome (1853) and in San Francisco (1893).

A Nemean revival

The Olympics are not the only ancient Greek games to have been re-established in modern times. In 1994, to mark the opening of the site of the Nemean sanctuary as an archaeological park, the Society for the Revival of the Nemean Games set up a new festival consisting solely of two contests, a 100-metre and a 7.5-kilometre foot-race, with the clay surface of the track and the starting gate authentically reconstructed. The contests are open to those of all ages and occupations, with no qualifications or training necessary; the competitors run bare-foot, though unlike their ancient predecessors they do not compete nude but in short tunics – a concession to modern reserve. The organizers warn the runners that false starts would be met with the original punishment of flogging by the judges, but no one seems to have warranted this retribution!

A new beginning

Jesse Owens (1913–80), the American track and field athlete who excelled in the sprint, hurdles and long jump. In May 1935 he broke six world records within 45 minutes. At the 1936 Berlin Olympics (shown here) he won four gold medals. The Nazi leader Adolf Hitler is reported to have said, 'The Americans should be ashamed of themselves, letting Negroes win medals for them. I shall not shake hands with this Negro.'

As discussed in the final chapter, the modern Olympics have been held every year with the exception of 1916, 1940 and 1944, when war intervened. Since 1924 there have been separate Winter Olympics, with the Winter and Summer Games being held two years apart since 1994. Nowadays, some 10,000 athletes take part, competing in over 200 disciplines. The Games are a far cry from their humble origins, but perhaps the ancient Greeks would not be surprised: the Olympics grew and evolved so much during the thousand years of their ancient history that it would perhaps be incredible at the coming of the third millennium for them to closely resemble their hallowed forerunners.

If the Olympic Games were being held now . . . you would be able to see for yourself why we attach such great importance to athletics. No-one can describe in mere words the extraordinary . . . pleasure derived from them and which you yourself would enjoy if you were seated among the spectators feasting your eyes on the prowess and stamina of the athletes, the beauty and power of their bodies, their incredible dexterity and skill, their invincible strength, their courage, ambition, endurance and tenacity. You would never stop . . . applauding them.

(Lucian, 2nd century AD, *Anacharsis* 12)

10 THE OLYMPIC GAMES SINCE 1896

After their auspicious if modest beginnings in Athens in 1896, the modern Olympic Games were slow to achieve the international prominence that Coubertin had hoped for. Although he was able to forestall the attempts by the Greeks to keep the fledgling Games in Greece on a permanent basis, their next celebration, in Paris in 1900, was less than auspicious.

Coubertin hoped that by making the Games a part of the Paris 1900 Universal Exposition it would enhance public awareness and help propel the Games onto the world stage. But he had miscalculated; far from boosting their reputation, they became no more than a sideshow to the Exposition. Coubertin lost control of the events, and they became a shambolic series of contests lasting throughout the summer. Many competitors and even winners would go to their graves not even realizing that they had taken part in an Olympic Games. Statisticians and historians continue to this day to debate which of the wide range of events, as diverse as obstacle-race swimming and ballooning, were or were not part of the Games.

The embryonic Games fared little better in 1904. The political and financial realities of major event management and international rivalry were already threatening Coubertin's idealistic ambitions, just as they had

Start of the first modern Olympic 100 metres final at the 1896 Games. After a gap of more than 100 years the Games are returning to Athens in 2004.

Dorando Pietri crosses the finishing line in London's White City stadium at the end of the 1908 Olympic marathon. Pietri's brave attempt to finish won him many admirers, but not a gold medal: the help given to him by well-meaning officials led to his disqualification.

bedevilled the ancient Games. After an initial decision by the International Olympic Committee to award the Games to Chicago, it later decided to move them to St Louis to coincide with the 1904 world fair, the Louisiana Purchase Exposition. The move, led by James Sullivan, a fierce rival of Coubertin, had been supported by US president Theodore Roosevelt. Coubertin declined to attend, as did all but a few athletes from outside North America. Again, the Games became an almost comical collection of events, from the more recognizable, such as track and field, to the highly unusual, such as pole climbing and roque (a variant of croquet), and once more were no more than an entertaining adjunct to a world fair.

Coubertin's vision was fading: he desperately needed to rediscover the euphoria of 1896. Help came from the enthusiastic Greeks who offered to stage an event in 1906 in Athens. Although initially reluctant to agree, fearing another Greek attempt to wrest control of the Games, Coubertin finally endorsed them. However, he denied them the official status of 'Olympic Games' and they became the 'Intercalated' or 'Interim' Games. He also chose not to attend, preferring to stay in Paris to organize an Olympic Congress to plan the 'Incorporation of the Fine Arts in the Olympic Games and in Everyday Life'. Ironically, the Games were a notable success: they breathed new life into the Olympic Movement and may well have saved it from looming extinction.

London was not the initial choice for the Games of the IV Olympiad in 1908. Rome had been granted the honour, but when Mount Vesuvius erupted in 1906, the Italian government said that scarce resources should be directed towards the rebuilding of Naples. Laudable as this sounds, it may well have been a convenient excuse as there is strong evidence that political intrigues within Italy had already denied the city of Rome the national finance that it needed. The British Olympic Association responded with great vigour. The Olympic Games, Greek in origin, reinvented by a Frenchman, would be celebrated in the land which either invented or codified most of the sports which make up the modern Olympic programme. Already famous sporting venues would be used: tennis at Wimbledon and Queens, shooting at Bisley, rowing at Henley, polo at Hurlingham; but, most significantly, a magnificent new stadium would be built to celebrate the majority of events, including swimming and track and field. The stadium became known as White City in Shepherd's Bush and could seat 63,000 spectators. Years ahead of its time, it could hold soccer, swimming, cycling, gymnastics and wrestling events simultaneously.

There were significant athletic performances to match the luxurious facilities, but the most notable drama occurred in the marathon. When Italian runner Dorando Pietri entered the stadium at the end of the 26-mile course, he was well ahead of the field. But he was exhausted and collapsed several times on the track before being helped across the line by well-meaning officials. This led to his disqualification, the gold medal going instead to the American Johnny Hayes. The finish was captured by the newsreel cameras. The story caught the public's imagination around the world and helped create the romantic mythology that is the essence of Olympic competition. Although there had been intense political rivalry at the Games, particularly between the British organizers and Coubertin's erstwhile adversary and leader of the US team James Sullivan, they were a great success. Over 2,000 athletes had participated (although only 2 per cent of them were women) from 22 nations.

Jim Thorpe putting the shot in the Olympic decathlon at the 1912 Stockholm Games. When the King of Sweden awarded him his gold medal he said to Thorpe, 'Sir, you are the greatest athlete in the world.' Thorpe is reported as replying, 'Thanks, King.'

The 1912 Games in Stockholm built on the success of London and became an organizational model for years to come. The Swedes were blessed with fine weather, and Coubertin, who had at last managed to introduce fine arts events into the Games (and who in fact won a gold medal for poetry under a pseudonym), must have felt that the much-lauded summer festival of mind and body typical of the ancient Games had returned much as he had hoped it would. Unfortunately, the biggest story of the Games was again that of an athlete's disappointment. Jim Thorpe, a Native American from the United States, may well be the greatest athlete of all time: he won both the pentathlon and decathlon to huge acclaim. However, the IOC followed the strict establishment tradition of the time: that noble sporting competition was the preserve of the gentleman amateur, not the professional tradesman. When it was discovered that Thorpe had earlier played Minor League Baseball for money, he was stripped of his medals. His titles and his medals

would not be reinstated until many years later, long after his death in poverty and obscurity.

Even more tragically, just as Coubertin's dream began to achieve reality, the horror of the Great War led to the cancellation of the 1916 Games and an end to much of the optimism of the Olympic cause. But the IOC managed, with some dignity, to forge a new spirit from the ravages of war. Antwerp in Belgium hosted the 1920 Games in recognition of its suffering during the war. The Olympic flag, symbolic of all the flags of all the nations of the world, appeared for the first time, as did the athletes' oath – spoken on this occasion by Belgium's Victor Boin, already a medallist in water polo in 1908 and 1912, who would win a silver in the team épée fencing event.

The noble efforts of the Belgians laid the foundations for a much bigger Games in Paris in 1924. Over 1,000 journalists attended, along with a multitude of

The inauguration of the athletes' oath at the Antwerp Games opening ceremony, 1920. Victor Boin of Belgium takes the oath on behalf of all the athletes at the Games. It became a symbol of the athletes' commitment to the Olympic ideal of fair and equal competition. The same oath is also taken by a representative of the judges and officials.

newsreel cameras. An inaugural winter festival, which would become the first Olympic Winter Games, had been held in Chamonix in February and set the scene for Paris later in the year. The Paris Games would be latterly dubbed the Games of the *Chariots of Fire* as the exploits of Britain's Eric Liddell and Harold Abrahams were re-created on celluloid in 1981. But at the time the stars of the Games were Paavo Nurmi, the great Finnish distance runner, Ville Ritola, his compatriot, and the American swimmer Johnny Weissmuller who converted his prowess in the Olympic pool into fame in Hollywood's Tarzan movies.

The growing success of the Games was consolidated at the Amsterdam Games of 1928 despite the controversy over the state of exhaustion suffered by the women at the end of their inaugural 800-metre event. The furore

Harold Abrahams wins the 100 metres for Great Britain in 1924. The Paris Games of 1924 were an important success for the IOC and for Coubertin. The performances of the British athletics team, particularly Abrahams and Scotland's Eric Liddell, became the subject of the famous Hugh Hudson film Chariots of Fire *in 1981.*

Finland's Paavo Nurmi lights the Olympic flame at the Helsinki Games in 1952. A legendary figure in distance running, Nurmi had won nine gold medals between 1920 and 1928. These became the first Cold War Games with the first appearance of the mighty Soviet team, housed in a separate Olympic village. Its athletes performed admirably, particularly the female gymnasts who began a forty-year winning streak.

which ensued within the male-dominated sporting hierarchy led to women's races longer than 200 metres being banned for the next thirty-two years. The Los Angeles Games of 1932 were also a popular success despite the exigencies of the Depression.

The principles of Olympism and the harsh realities of the twentieth century met head-on at the Berlin Games of 1936. Although Berlin had been chosen long before Adolf Hitler came to power, the Olympic Movement did little to resist the open abuse and manipulation of the Games by Germany's Nazi regime. Some would argue that the performances of Jesse Owens and other African-Americans represented a sufficient symbolic denouncement of Nazi propaganda to suggest that it was the Olympic spirit that emerged the stronger from the unfortunate spectacle of swastikas and Nazi salutes. Others would argue that it was the worst moment in Olympic history, especially if cast in the ironic light of the appalling discrimination that Owens and other Black Americans suffered on their return to the United States.

The 1936 Berlin Games would be the last for twelve years as the Second World War engulfed Europe and eventually the whole world. They would also be Coubertin's final Games, not that he would witness them. His family fortune gone, spent in large part on his work for the Olympic Movement, he had been living in seclusion in Lausanne, where he died in 1937.

The rapidly changing post-war world was reflected in a rapidly changing Olympic Games. London once again organized a Games in less-than-favourable circumstances. Rationing and bomb damage were all too evident in a war-ravaged city. But the Games were a success, especially for the 'Flying Dutchwoman' Fanny Blankers-Koen, who became the first woman to be acknowledged as the star of the Games.

The Summer Games became truly global as, in succession, they travelled to Helsinki, Rome, Tokyo and Mexico City. They also became huge global media events as television began to make its indelible mark. At first, it seemed to be no more than a modest window on proceedings; it wasn't until later that its more profound influence would be felt.

From the 1950s, Olympic competition started to become a weapon of the Cold War rivalry between East and West that would eventually lead to major political boycotts, in 1980 in Moscow and in 1984 in Los Angeles. The Games also became a focus of protest over South African Apartheid that led to a major African boycott in 1976 in Montreal. However, the oxygen of publicity provided by television led to the most harrowing incident in the history

of the Games in Munich in 1972. Ten days into the celebration of the Games, eight Palestinian terrorists broke into the Olympic village and took hostage several members of the Israeli team. In the ensuing hours, seventeen people were killed. Following a memorial service, the IOC decided that the Games should continue. The wisdom of its decision will be long debated.

For the Olympic Movement the 1970s and 1980s were dark days. It faced seemingly implacable problems: terrorism, political boycotts, lack of moral authority and financial paucity of ominous proportions. Many critics suggested that the Games had no future, either in pragmatic terms, or in terms of ethical values. However, in 1980 a diminutive and wily Spaniard, Juan Antonio Samaranch, possessed of significant personal ambition, strong commercial acumen and shrewd political guile, became president of the IOC. Over the following twenty years of his tenure the Games overcame most of their practical problems, if not all their ethical ones. The hypocrisy of sham amateurism was confronted as professionalism was embraced. Commercial sponsorship was welcomed so that financial security could be ensured. Political boycotts were ended as the IOC learned how to play the game of international diplomacy. The Olympic Games, most notably Barcelona in 1992 and Lillehammer in 1994, became spectacular celebrations of human achievement and aspiration. At long last the Games became at least

The spectacle of the Olympic Games opening ceremony in Sydney, 2000. These Games were a major success for the Australian organizers and for the IOC.

as significant in the modern world as they had been in ancient times, if not more so. Equally, the heroes of the modern Games became as revered (and rewarded) as their predecessors in the ancient Games. But there was to be a sting in the tail: as history often proves, success can breed conceit and money can breed corruption.

The greatest scandal to befall the Olympic Movement occurred in 1999. Rumours circulating for many years about the corrupt behaviour of several members of the IOC were confirmed when it was disclosed that leading officials of the organizing committee for the Salt Lake City Olympic Winter Games of 2002 had bribed several IOC members to gain their votes in its successful bid to become the host city of the Games. Samaranch's time in office was seriously tarnished. For a while, his days seemed numbered, as did those of the IOC itself. But he remained in power to oversee a thorough overhaul of the bidding city election process and a full review of the ethical behaviour of the IOC membership.

There followed two highly successful and popular games: Sydney in 2000 and Salt Lake City in 2002. Significantly, a new IOC president was elected in Moscow in 2001. Jacques Rogge, a highly respected Belgian surgeon, will have to continue to convince the world that the IOC is once again worthy of its position in the vanguard of world sport. Rogge will also have to confront the biggest moral threat of all: the widespread use of performance-enhancing drugs. A significant problem since at least the 1950s, cheating through the use of drugs threatens the ethical underpinnings of the Games

Ben Johnson wins the 100-metre men's sprint in Seoul, 1988. Johnson was later stripped of the title after testing positive for a banned anabolic steroid, Stanozolol. Several other finalists from the same race, including Carl Lewis, Linford Christie and Denis Mitchell, were later involved in drugs allegations.

and of sport itself. For many years, only superficial and cosmetic measures were employed to combat their use. However, in 1999 the IOC established the World Anti-Doping Agency to deal with the crisis. The current official line from the WADA and the IOC is that the battle is being won. Contrary to this, the widely held belief within world public opinion is that, at best, the jury is still out. The future of the Games awaits the outcome.

However, despite these recent issues, the modern Games have become a remarkable spectacle, both as a global event on an unparalleled scale and as a testament to human endeavour and idealism. The Games are now held to almost universal acclaim, 200 nations participate, and an Olympic truce is declared, just as in ancient times, for the duration of the Games. On the whole, the world's athletes do compete in the spirit of fair and equal competition, just as Pierre de Coubertin hoped they would. Olympism has come to represent a set of values at the core of sporting competition that has great philosophical significance, both culturally and educationally. Were the ancient Greek originators of the Games to return to witness the modern Games, they might well be both gratified and proud of what they saw.

FURTHER READING

Olympia and the Olympic Games

W. Coulson, H. Kyrieleis (eds), *Proceedings of an International Symposium on the Olympic Games*, 1988, Deutsches Archäologisches Institut, Athens 1992

L. Drees, *Olympia: Gods, Artists and Athletes*, English translation, Pall Mall Press, London 1968

M.I. Finley, H.W. Pleket, *The Olympic Games: The First Thousand Years*, Chatto & Windus, London 1975

H.-V. Herrmann, *Olympia: Heiligtum und Wettkampfstätte*, Hirmer Verlag, Munich 1972

H.M. Lee, *The Program and Schedule of the Ancient Olympic Games*, Weidman, Hildesheim 2001 (*Nikephoros*, Beihefte, Bd. 6)

A. Mallwitz, H.-V. Herrmann (eds), *Die Funde aus Olympia*, Deutsches Archäo-logisches Institut, Verlag S. Kasas, Athens 1980

A. Mallwitz, *Olympia und seine Bauten*, Prestel-Verlag, Munich 1972

W.J. Raschke (ed.), *The Archaeology of the Olympics: The Olympics and Other Festivals in Antiquity*, University of Wisconsin Press, Madison 1988

E. Spathari, *The Olympic Spirit*, Adam Editions, Athens 1992

A. & N. Yalouris, *Olympia: the Museum and the Sanctuary*, Ekdotike Athenon S.A., Athens 1987

Modern Olympics

F. Burns, *Heigh for Cotswold! A History of Robert Dover's Olympic Games*, Robert Dover's Games Society, Chipping Campden 1981

F. Burns, 'Robert Dover's Cotswold Olympick Games: the use of the term "Olimpick"', *Olympic Review* 201 (1985), pp. 230–6

S. Greenberg, *Olympic Facts and Figures*, Guinness Publishing, London 1996

D. Wallechinsky, *The Complete Book of the Olympics*, Penguin, London 1995

Exhibition catalogues

Olympism in Antiquity, vols I–III, ed. D. Vanhove, catalogues of loan exhibitions to the Olympic Museum, Lausanne, 1993, 1996, 1998

Arte y Olimpismo, ed. J. Artigues, I. Rebassa, P. Llull and I. Llobera, Fundación 'La Caixa', 1999 (Palma, Oviéu, Las Palmas de Gran Canaria 1999/2000)

Mind and Body: Athletic Contests in Ancient Greece, National Archaeological Museum, Athens 1989–90, Ministry of Culture/The National Hellenic Committee, I.C.O.M., 1989

Le sport dans la Grèce antique: du jeu à la compétition, ed. D. Vanhove, Palais des Beaux-Arts, Brussels 1992

Sport in der Antike: Wettkampf, Spiel und Erziehung im Altertum, ed. U. Sinn, Martin-von-Wagner-Museum, Würzburg, Ergon Verlag, 1996

Ancient sport

M. Golden, *Sport and Society in Ancient Greece*, Cambridge University Press, 1998

H.A. Harris, *Greek Athletes and Athletics*, Hutchinson, London 1964/University of Indiana Press, Bloomington 1966

H.A. Harris, *Sport in Greece and Rome*, Thames & Hudson, London 1972

E. Kefalidou, *The Victorious Athlete: A Study on the Iconography of Ancient Greek Athletics*, Aristotle University of Thessaloniki, 1966 [in Greek with short English summary]

D.G. Kyle, *Athletics in Ancient Athens*, E.J. Brill, Leiden 1987

D. Sansone, *Greek Athletics and the Genesis of Sport*, University of California Press, Berkeley and Los Angeles, 1988

T.F. Scanlon, *Greek and Roman Athletics: A Bibliography*, Ares Publishers Inc., Chicago 1984

W. Sweet, *Sport and Recreation in Ancient Greece*, Oxford University Press, 1987

D.C. Young, *The Olympic Myth of Greek Amateur Athletics*, Chicago 1985

Medical aspects

R. Jackson, *Doctors and Diseases in the Roman Empire*, British Museum Press, London 1991

G. Penso, *La médecine romaine, L'art d'Esculape dans la Rome antique*, Les Éditions R. Dacosta, Paris 1984

E.D. Phillips, *Aspects of Greek Medicine*, Croom Helm, London and Sydney 1987 (first published as *Greek Medicine*, Thames & Hudson, London 1973)

S. Retsas, 'Medicine and the Olympic Games in Antiquity' in *Proceedings of the 1st International Medical Olympiad (Kos Island 1996)*, Athens 1996, pp. 25–33

ACKNOWLEDGEMENTS

Grateful thanks are due to the following. Kim Allen made the model of Olympia from working drawings by Sue Bird, who also provided the artwork for the first edition of this book. The original drawings were revised and new ones created for this edition by Candida Lonsdale. Philip Nicholls took most of the British Museum photographs. Hans Ruprecht Goette and Klaus Herrmann assisted with photographs from the Deutsches Archäologisches Institut in Athens; Jürgen Schilbach, also of the DAI, helped with information regarding the site. Information on coins was supplied by Philip Attwood, Andy Meadows and Janet Larkin (British Museum Department of Coins & Medals). Francis Burns (Cotswold Olimpick Society) provided information about the English revivals, and Jan Paterson and Rebecca Middleton of the British Olympic Association, Education Trust, about the modern Olympics. Most notably regarding the modern Games, Stewart Binns has generously contributed the new last chapter for the 2004 edition. Secretarial and general assistance came from Joan Edwards, Marian Vian, Carol Cosgrove, Prem Bhudia, Neil Adams and Jonathan Lloyd. Peter Higgs has shared and discussed ideas about antiquities, and Ralph Jackson about ancient medicine (both British Museum). Dyfri Williams (British Museum) and Susan Woodford read and made suggestions on the text, as did Stephen Instone (University College London), who acted as consultant regarding modern parallels for the ancient events, and my husband, Robert Broomfield, who also took many of the site photographs. The book was edited by Colin Grant and designed by Martin Richards.

ILLUSTRATION SOURCES AND CREDITS

Illustrations are listed by page number. Unless otherwise stated, all objects illustrated are in the British Museum, and the Museum registration and/or catalogue numbers are given here where applicable. Photographs of British Museum objects including the model of Olympia were provided by the Museum Photographic Service. Line drawings and maps (on pp. 9b, 11, 12, 13t, 14, 16, 18t, 20, 21l, 31t, 37, 52, 59b, 66, 67b, 69b, 77) were done by Candida Lonsdale, Department of Greek and Roman Antiquities, British Museum.

1 GR 1776.11-8.2/Sculpture 1736
2 GR 1836.2-24.193/Vase B 133
4–5 Klaus Herrmann, Deutsches Archäologisches Institut
8 GR 1865.1-3.36/Bronze 909
9t Museum of Olympia
9b GR 1849.5-18.3/Vase E 262
10t Coin Elis 72
10b GR 1824.4-99.17/Bronze 264
13b Notebook of Sir William Gell describing the Dilettanti Mission to Asia Minor 1811/12
15b A. Loxias, Piraeus
17bl & br Robert Broomfield
18b Coin Elis 160
20 Museum of Olympia
21l Museum of Olympia
21r Robert Broomfield
22t Robert Broomfield
22b *Olympia: Die Ergebnisse der von dem deutschen Reich veranstalteten Ausgrabung,* hrsg. E. Curtius und F. Adler, 1896, Tafelband II, T. CXV
24 Robert Broomfield
25 CM 1866.12-1.1028
28b *Olympia: Die Ergebnisse der von dem deutschen Reich veranstalteten Ausgrabung,* hrsg. E. Curtius und F. Adler, 1896, Tafelband II, T. CXII
29 Robert Broomfield

30 Athens, National Archaeological Museum 15499, Hellenic Republic, Ministry of Culture
31 Robert Broomfield
32 Robert Broomfield
35t GR 1869.2-5.3/Vase E 83
39 GR 1988.10-20.2
40 GR 1867.5-8.1119/Vase E 342
42 GR 1876.5-10.1/Bronze 208
44 GR 1867.5-8.968/Vase B295
45t Biblioteca Medicea Laurenziana, Florence
45b GR 1865.7-12.94/Gem 730
48t GR 1907.10-20.2
48b GR 1868.1-5.46/Bronze 2455
49 GR 1857.8-7.1/Sculpture 1754
51 GR 1867.5-8.1139/Vase E 164
54 GR 1839.2-14.68/Vase E 455
55l GR 1856.12-26.220
55r GR 1873.8-20.154/Bronze 881
56 GR 1856.10-1.1/Vase B 609
57 GR 1864.10-7.156
58 helmet GR 1904.10-10.2, greaves GR 1856.12-26.710/Bronze 2860
59t GR 1836.2-24.173/Vase E 818
59b GR 1873.8-20.369/Vase B 608
60 Robert Broomfield
61l GR 1772.3-20.381/Vase E 629
61r GR 1856.12-26.779/Bronze 223
63 GR 1898.7-16.3/Bronze 3207
64 GR 1814.7-4.43/Sculpture 250
65 Coin Cos 8
67t GR 1842.3-14.1/Vase B 134
68 GR 1843.2-16.2/Vase B 35
69t GR 1847.8-6.26/Vase B 48
70t GR 1837.6-9.83
70b GR 1867.5-6.48
72 GR 1843.11-3.69/Vase B 271
73 GR 1824.4-27.1/Bronze 1614
74t GR 1836.2-24.196/Vase E 94
74b GR 1928.1-17.59
75 GR 1850.3-2.2/Vase E 78
76t GR 1836.2-24.105/Vase B 494
76b Coin Alexandria 1054
77t Athens, National Archaeological Museum AIG 2548 (Dimitriou Collection), Hellenic Republic,

Ministry of Culture
77b Rome, Museo delle Terme 1055
78t GR 1846.5-12.2/Vase E 6
78b GR 1897.4-1.1287/Vase C 334
79 GR 1852.4-1.1-2/ Terracottas D85 and D84
80 GR 1888.11-15.5/Vase B 607
83 GR 1867.5-8.743/Bronze 960
84t GR 1866.4-15.249/Vase B 606
84b GR 1865.7-12.102/Gem 679
85t GR 1894.10-30.1/Bronze 2695
85b GR 1880.12-11.1/Bronze 253/ GR 1902.9-16.1 (right)
86 GR 1843.11-3.82/Vase B 304
87 Coin 1946.1-1.1084
88 GR 1849.11-22.1/Vase B 144
89t Athens, National Archaeological Museum 15177, Hellenic Republic, Ministry of Culture
89b GR 1873.8-20.262
90 GR 1864.10-21.4/Sculpture 501
91t GR 1843.11-3.53/Vase E 52
91b GR 1874.7-10.347/Gem 1198
92t GR 1836.2-24.212/Vase E 70
92b GR 1836.2-24.114/Vase E 37
93 GR 1859.12-26.19/ Inscription 928
96 GR 1823.6-10.1/Bronze 250
97 Athens, National Archaeological Museum 4464, Hellenic Republic, Ministry of Culture
98 Athens, National Archaeological Museum X6164, Hellenic Republic, Ministry of Culture
100 Robert Broomfield
101 Olympic Museum, Lausanne
102 Robert Broomfield
103t GR 2001.5-8.1
103b CM 1912.10-4.1
104 British Library
105 British Library
106 IOC/Allsport
107-14 Getty Images

INDEX